A Lap of the Globe

A Lap of the Globe

Behind the Wheel of a Vintage Mercedes in the World's Longest Auto Race

KEVIN CLEMENS

FOREWORD BY FRANK BARRETT

McFarland & Company, Inc., Publishers
Jefferson, North Carolina, and London

LIBRARY OF CONGRESS CATALOGUING-IN-PUBLICATION DATA

Clemens, Kevin, 1957–
    A lap of the globe : behind the wheel of a vintage Mercedes in the world's longest auto race / Kevin Clemens ; foreword by Frank Barrett.
        p.   cm.
    Includes index.

    ISBN-13: 978-0-7864-2561-7
    ISBN-10: 0-7864-2561-X
    (softcover : 50# alkaline paper) ∞

    1. Around the Word in 80 Days Motor Challenge (Automobile race) (2000)   2. Clemens, Kevin, 1957–   — Travel.   3. Voyages around the world.   I. Title.
    GV1029.2.C56 2006
    796.72–dc22   2006020689

British Library cataloguing data are available

On the cover: The imposing front grille of a 1959 Mercedes-Benz 220S sedan; globe by Photospin.com.

Manufactured in the United States of America

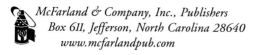
McFarland & Company, Inc., Publishers
Box 611, Jefferson, North Carolina 28640
www.mcfarlandpub.com

To Jessica and Jeremy
and a life filled with adventure

Table of Contents

Foreword by Frank Barrett

Millions of people can visualize a trip around the world, but few of us can actually make such a bold adventure happen. Most folks would fly or sail around the globe, but a few crazies drive—or try to. Of those hardy few, most choose the latest and greatest off-road vehicle. Nobody sane would even try to make the trip in a 40-year-old sedan. Nobody with any common sense would pay well over $100,000 to abuse themselves and their old car for 80 days in the worst possible driving conditions. But Kevin did. We're not sure what that says about him, but we're glad he took on the challenge. After all, somebody has to do the truly wacky things.

To help him succeed in this endurance contest, Kevin had an unusually broad automotive background as an engineer, journalist, restorer, and vintage racer. He also had the savvy to recognize that this round-the-world effort involved more than just shipping a car to the start line. He knew that finishing the grueling event would require years of preparation, a compatible co-driver, strong financial backing, and much more. He even hit me up for sponsorship!

Our link came through our mutual appreciation for old Mercedes-Benzes. Both of us owned 220 sedans of the late 1950s. These were among the most durable cars of their era—definitely not fast but stout, safe, and relatively easy to diagnose and repair. If you had been driving around the world in 1959, you'd probably have chosen the same car that Kevin picked—in his words, a "somewhat frumpy" 1959 220S. Given the tough conditions, he was smart enough to choose a model that was relatively simple and had been common in its day, so if he needed a part in, say, Turkey, he might be able to find it in a junkyard. Turns out, that was exactly what happened.

Kevin also found an innocent co-driver, Dr. Mark Rinkel, a dentist. Maybe Kevin figured the rigors of the trip would serve as revenge for all the time he'd spent suffering in a dentist's chair. You'll have to ask Mark about that.

The dirty little secret of the world of automotive journalism is that most writers never get their hands dirty working on cars, and some don't even own a car, let alone a vintage model. But Kevin is different. He's that almost unheard-of combination of journalist, engineer, writer, photographer, and mechanic. While actually coaxing his 40-year-old horse around the world, he found the time and energy to write about and photograph his experience for readers of *The Star*, the national magazine of the Mercedes-Benz Club of America. Thanks to an early Nikon digital camera and the Internet, he was able to send periodic dispatches to the magazine from waypoints along the route. Reading about the experience was far easier than doing it.

Although the team was well prepared, they got off to a tough start, with repairs for an accident and a failed head gasket proving that Kevin had made a wise choice of cars. More importantly, though, these trials proved the team's determination. While any sensible person would have given up and headed home, Kevin was in a truck in Istanbul looking for a guy with some old Mercedes-Benz parts. Thanks to him, the team kept going.

One day in June 2000, Kevin sent us a pleading e-mail. The car's transmission was failing, and to finish the event he desperately needed a replacement. Since I owned a similar car and had a few contacts, I glibly offered to find him one. Expecting to endure a long search, I was surprised that just three local phone calls found three gearboxes nearby. I quickly bought one and took it to Denver's best mechanic for old Mercedes-Benzes, Mark Langston at Stu Ritter Inc., to check it out. After Mark pronounced it fit and poured in fresh lubricant, a friend and I stuck it in my 300TE wagon and headed 700 miles north to meet Kevin in Bozeman, Montana.

One of the first sights we saw at the headquarters motel was Claude Picasso's 230SL, lightly rolled the day before. Claude had reportedly paid Mercedes-Benz something north of $200,000 to prep the car, and unfortunately much of the work had come undone in a few seconds on a dirt road outside Shelby, Montana. Sometimes things just don't work out the way you've planned.

Before dinner with Kevin and Mark at an Italian place in Bozeman, I had the chance to drive Kevin's car. What a mess! The poor old thing had been well and truly hammered within an inch of its life. Even at moderate speeds it moaned and shook like an old dog and steered about as well. When Kevin asked me what I thought was wrong, it was hard to think of anything that was right! But the faithful 220S was still running, and that's all that really mattered.

Next morning we followed the team southward over dirt roads to Gardner, Montana, then into Yellowstone National Park, where we managed to shoot a few photos and watch them handle some adversity. When a front wheel bearing promptly gave up the ghost, Kevin simply pulled over, replaced it, and was on his way again in minutes. No big deal.

Held in the centenary year, this was the first-ever truly round-the-world rally. Evidently the 1908 New York to Paris race had been frightening enough to deter imitators for the following 90 years. Only the British would organize an event this masochistic. In fact, given today's global political conditions, this event probably slipped through just before the borders closed in several volatile countries.

Will the event ever be repeated? Don't hold your breath. The timing of this event was fortuitous. It's unlikely to be repeated for any kind of car, let alone old ones. Thanks to Kevin, you can enjoy the experience from the comfort of your chair, so read on.

Frank Barrett is the editor and publisher of The Star, *Mercedes-Benz Club of America.*

Preface

Mine is the perfect life for a car guy. After earning bachelor's and master's degrees in materials engineering from Rensselaer Polytechnic Institute, I went to work at Michelin Tire's Research and Development Center in Greenville, South Carolina.

At Michelin I designed high-performance and racing tires and worked as a corporate public relations counselor. But I eventually left that life and became an automotive journalist. My work has appeared in magazines and newspapers like *Automobile, European Car, The Star* and *Reader's Digest*. For a person who likes cars and loves to travel, it is a dream job. It also has given me a chance to meet a variety of interesting people. Although the auto business is huge, the number of people who make things happen is fairly small, and it has been my privilege to meet many of them. It also has meant that when I have come up with crazy schemes involving automobiles, I could usually find some like-minded soul in the industry to help me realize my dreams.

This constant dreaming is what led me to undertake the Around the World in 80 Days Motor Challenge. Never before had an automotive event circled the entire globe returning to its starting place, and I knew that I wanted to be a part of this historic adventure. I was aware of the 1908 New York to Paris epic contest that had been won by an American team of drivers, and perhaps that was part of my inspiration. Beyond that, I wanted to see parts of the world that "normal" travelers never get to visit. Travel by automobile, especially by old automobile, provides the traveler with a unique experience. The lack of air conditioning and creature comforts that drivers of more modern conveyances insist are vital are the very things that isolate you from the essence of travel. Old cars are leisurely, classy and fun and a really good way to literally see the world.

My Around the World adventure would not have been possible without the help, support and encouragement of a variety of companies and individuals. It is almost impossible to recognize everyone involved in the adventure, but I'll at least try to mention a few. The ones I inadvertently miss know me well enough to forgive me.

My wife, Loree Kalliainen, was a constant source of support and encouragement and a strong force behind this book. She saw me off when I left for the start in England, met me in Beijing, met me again in Bay City, Michigan, and finally came to the finish in London. She never complained when I woke her with calls from Uzbekistan or China at 3 a.m., and kept our life together and running smoothly while I was off on my three month adventure.

Mark Rinkel was my partner and co-driver in this endeavor. Mark is almost my complete opposite in every way, yet we formed a team that overcame adversity that would have stopped a lesser team. Mark is brave; he never let me know how frightened he was when we were clinging to a cliff side or sliding over goat trails at insane speeds. He worked just as hard as I did to drag our old Mercedes-Benz around the world and I would go with him again, given the chance.

Although every person on the event was special and the process of writing this book has brought back a variety of pleasant memories, there were a few individuals whose friendship made the drive even more enjoyable. Among them are Rich Newman and his daughter Julie, Peter and Ann Hunt, Will and Carrie Balfour, Pat and Mary Brooks, Bill and Kelly Secrest, Henning Ulrich and Klemens Suchocki, and Ed and Bev Suhrbier.

Among those in the corporate world who made my adventure possible, special thanks go to Steve Rossi (then with Mercedes-Benz), Maryalice Ritzmann (Mercedes-Benz), Susan Sizemore (Bridgestone Firestone), Dan Schmutte (then with TechSight), Frank Barrett (*The Star* magazine), Sherri Collins (then at *European Car* magazine) and a variety of others who sponsored us with products and moral support. I am forever grateful for your belief in our team. In addition the friendly presence of Tim Winker and Randy Jokela, both from Duluth, Minnesota, made the U.S. portion of our adventure go that much more smoothly. Several of their photos are included in this book.

Lastly, without the vision of Philip Young and the dedication of his hardworking Classic Rally Association team, none of this would have been possible. The timing crews, medical teams and especially the mechanics and crews of the sweep vehicles made it their personal goal to leave no vehicles behind, and they performed miracles keeping everyone on the road. Driving around the world, for them, was especially trying, but they met the challenge with good cheer and were just as much a part of the adventure as any of the competitors.

It was a journey beyond compare, and I hope that my efforts to bring it to you with this book will give you some flavor of this extraordinary adventure.

Kevin Clemens
Lake Elmo, Minnesota

1

Looking for Adventure

It didn't take long after the birth of the automobile before people began to wonder what these noisy and obnoxious contraptions could do. Initially, the completion of any journey of almost any length was considered an accomplishment. The first formal race or "reliability trial" was held in 1894 and went from Paris to Rouen, a distance of 79 miles. As cars grew more advanced and became slightly more reliable, and as covering distance became more certain, city to city races became the true test of automotive endurance. These were desperate affairs, leaving behind a trail of carnage and destruction. The rudimentary machines frequently killed their drivers and riding mechanics and occasionally mowed down ranks of spectators. Races were tamed eventually, being placed on closed road circuits, but the seeds of the adventure involved in driving long distances on the open highway were sown.

In 1904, the American Automobile Association (AAA) created a plan for a 1,350-mile tour from New York to the World's Fair in St. Louis, Missouri. The objective was to drive through different parts of the country to experience a variety of different road surfaces and driving conditions. Of the 77 cars that officially participated in the run, 66 made it to St. Louis. Among the participants, 36 different makes of automobile were represented, and the run took 18 days. The AAA sent out pilot cars ahead of the main body of the event and coordinated the participation of local motorists as the tour passed through their towns. The tour became a major media event as, until this time, the idea of the automobile as a long distance conveyance was nearly unthinkable. After the initial success, the AAA announced that the run would be repeated as a reliability and endurance tour with strict rules and an overall winner. Charles J. Glidden, a New England industrialist and automobilist, offered a $2,000 trophy, and from then on, the AAA

9

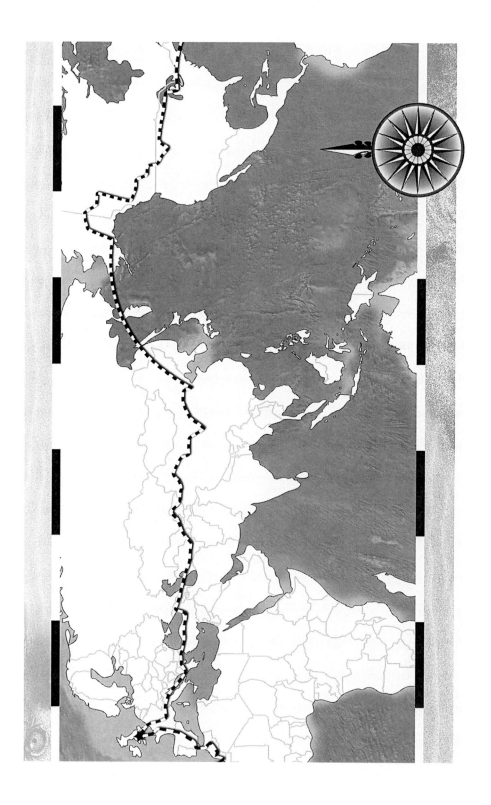

Finish of the Vanderbilt Cup Race on Long Island, New York, circa 1905. *Library of Congress*

tours became known as the Glidden Tours. The events were considered one of the most grueling tests for automobiles, and manufacturers took their participation very seriously. The Glidden Tours ended in 1913 as the reliability and performance of the automobile were no longer in doubt. A version of the Glidden Tour was revived in 1946 as a showcase for the burgeoning antique car hobby in America.

The success of the early Glidden Tours brought about a realization that the automobile could be used to cover long distances. To be certain, such long distance touring wasn't easy. Roads were still questionable and automotive technology was in its infancy, but the AAA had shown the world what was possible. Still, it was shocking when, in 1907, *Le Matin* newspaper in Paris asked: "Is there anyone who will undertake to travel this summer from Paris to Peking by automobile?" The proposal was met with incredulity. The concept seemed infeasible. There were no roads. There were no gas stations. There were the possibilities of hostile natives. Yet, in

Opposite: **Route of the Around the World in 80 Days Motor Challenge, 2000.** *Rebecca Rayman*

An early Glidden Tour visits Cincinnati, circa, 1905. *Library of Congress*

early June, five intrepid teams of motorists sat on the start line in Peking (the direction of the route had been reversed) ready to compete for glory or die in the attempt. The Italian Prince Scipio Borghese's Italia led from the start and finished in Paris in 60 days, a full three weeks ahead of the second place competitor. More significantly, aboard Borghese's Italia was journalist Luigi Barzini. His reports of the team's exploits, telegraphed into newspaper offices from the most remote places, allowed automobilists and adventurers around the globe to follow the action. After this most extraordinary adventure, Barzini's book *Peking to Paris* became an international best seller and a "bible" for young Italian men: a blueprint of how to live an adventurous life.

Hardly had the ink dried on Barzini's adventure tale when another, perhaps even more audacious, motoring challenge was made. *Le Matin* proposed a 20,000-mile race, from New York to Paris. *Incroyable!* And yet the romance of the idea couldn't be denied. The French newspaper eventually convinced the *New York Times* to come onboard as a sponsor, and a starting date of February 12, 1908, was set. Six cars left New York looking for adventure, fame and glory.

I understand the hunt for adventurer undertaken by the early motorists. I envy them. They lived in a time when adventure, especially automotive adventure, sat on their doorstep. Every journey was fraught with peril, mechanical mayhem and excitement. Today's cars have, thankfully, removed most of the drama from driving. Nobody wants to have their daily commute interrupted by mechanical problems or the uncertainty of marginal roads. Yet adventure is still possible in the modern world. My bookshelves are filled with stories of mountain climbers and sailors, explorers and their expeditions. Adventure won't come to find you. You have to look for adventure.

When I left the button-down world of engineering and started writing for *Automobile Magazine* in the early 1990s, my mentor was senior editor Kathleen Hamilton. She taught me the writing business. She showed me the difference between a good story and one that was bound to be dull. It took time, but I learned. It was worth it because I quickly discovered that the writing shtick was a lot more fun than having a real job.

One day, having returned from a press trip and turned in my story, Kathleen made a scathing accusation. "You are an adventurer who pays for

More than 250,000 people attended the start of the 1908 New York to Paris Race in 1908. *Courtesy of the Detroit Public Library, National Automotive History Collection*

his fun by going on a trip and then coming home and writing about it," she said, shaking her head sadly. "For a writer, the whole purpose of a trip should be to write about it." It took me a long time to figure out what she meant. Eventually, I began to look forward to a trip as an opportunity to write a story, rather than simply adventure. This was something new and I found reliving the adventure on the page was nearly as exciting as the experience had been. I was set to become that writer that Hamilton held in such high regard.

At the end of the millennium and just over 100 years after the invention of the automobile, forty teams of slightly mad motorists from all over the world were planning to set out on a motorized competition from London with the intent to circumnavigate the globe in classic automobiles. To add some romance, the goal was to complete this journey in the 80 days specified by the incomparable dreamer and writer Jules Verne.

Jules Verne's adventurous traveler, Philias Phogg, was an English gentleman in the finest Victorian tradition. He was rich, articulate, reclusive and distinctly upper crust, exactly the type of entrant that the organizers of a latter-day classic car rally around the world would want to attract. I am not rich, and my crust is not upper, but I knew I would have to go. I signed on to test my mettle as a competitor and adventurer, and to bring back the story as a writer. Deep down, I also wanted to win. I knew I would try to win, even as I tried to convince everyone, including myself, that I was doing it to get the story.

Regardless of how it worked out, I knew it would be something that would stay with me the rest of my life. It's a cliché that I hate, but it really would be a once in a lifetime opportunity. I have found that having done something is often far better than actually doing it. The warm glow of accomplishment replaces the memories of misery and desperation that often surround things that are worthwhile and difficult. I suspected driving around the world would be this way.

First, I needed to learn about the history of the classic car rally. In 1997, Philip Young and the Classic Rally Association in England created the Peking to Paris Motor Challenge, loosely based upon the epic 1907 Peking to Paris race from a hundred years earlier. Young had convinced a hundred owners of classic automobiles to pay him enormous sums of money necessary to organize such an adventure. The logistics were a nightmare as the route included China, Tibet, Nepal, India, and Iran, where the locals aren't always friendly to westerners. But Philip Young pulled it off, creating an extraordinary event that elevated him to the status of legend among the small number of people who organize such international classic car rallies for the lucky few who can afford them.

There were three major organizations, and a few smaller ones in the business of producing large-scale classic car rallies. Most were British, which says something about the daft spirit of adventure still present in that island nation. Phillip Young is generally given credit for starting the classic endurance rally concept with the Pirelli Marathon Rally in 1989. He has since gone on to re-create rallies based upon a Monte Carlo event from the 1950s and various other marathon rallies from the 1960s. Young especially likes sturdy pre–War cars and mundane sedans from the 1950s, and that is the type of vehicles he tries to attract. His events run on regular roads with competitors often dodging local traffic. With the volume of traffic increasing even in remote parts of Europe, people wonder every year how much longer he can keep putting on these events. Belligerent, moody and difficult to talk with one-on-one, Young becomes a dynamo in front of a large crowd. After his success with Peking to Paris, most doubted that anyone could do an event that would top it.

Two other major rally organizers provided variations on the Classic Rally Association's theme. Nick Brittan's Trans World Events catered more to cars from the 1960s and 1970s. His events featured closed roads where competitors run flat out against the clock in competition-prepared cars to determine a winner. Brittan also recreated classic events, mostly from the sixties, such as the London to Sydney and London to Mexico World Cup events Brittan's events were: faster and frequently more dangerous than the others, and competitors rank them as comparable in value to Phillip Young's and note that Brittan — unlike Young — is friendly and approachable.

John Brown was the third major purveyor of classic car good times, primarily known for his Land's End to John O'Groats (LeJOG) event, which takes place in December. Brown's Historic Endurance Rally Organization (HERO) runs events on open roads and also caters to early pre–War cars. The competition side of a John Brown rally is quite intense, and Brown himself is fairly reclusive.

As 1997 ended, all three organizers began to look at unique ways to celebrate the upcoming turn of the century and the new millennium. Nick Brittan was first out of the box when he announced he would again re-create the 1968 London to Sydney Rally in time to coincide with the 2000 Summer Olympics in Australia. This caught my attention. The whole idea of rallying had been formed in my adolescent brain when, as a teenager, I read former Grand Prix racer Innes Ireland's madcap 1971 book *Sideways to Sydney*, in which he recounts his adventures in the original 1968 event. Ireland's ride for that event was a privately prepared Mercedes-Benz sedan.

Before the ink was dry on that announcement, Philip Young made an even more audacious proclamation. He would organize a classic car event in the year 2000 that would literally circle the globe. The Around the World in 80 Days Motor Challenge would have everything. Although a westward race from New York to Paris had taken place in 1908, no competitive motor-sports event had ever actually gone all the way around the world, returning to the exact spot from which it had started. But this was exactly what the pugnacious Philip Young was proposing. It had people immediately doubting that he could ever pull it off.

I first learned about Philip Young's 1997 Peking to Paris event through the pages of several of the British classic car magazines. I followed the event's progress on the Internet as teams struggled through landslides and flooded rivers, running against the clock in an effort to avoid time penalties. It was on the Internet that I also learned of the death of a German competitor and his 17-year-old son; they had crashed into a truck with their souped-up VW Beetle.

In spite of these dangers, or maybe because of them, I envied the teams that fought their way halfway around the world to finish triumphantly in Paris. I promised myself that I would be a competitor and not an Internet bystander on Young's drive around the world.

George Schuster, a factory test driver for the Thomas Motor Company in Buffalo, won the 1908 New York to Paris event, competing against teams from Europe. Remarkably, in 1966, fifty-eight years after his triumph, George Schuster wrote a book with Tom Mahoney describing the 1908 event (*The Longest Auto Race*, The John Day Company). The race described by Schuster had been epic in its difficulties, and the route had changed almost daily due to political concerns and organizational problems. That event had taken 170 days to complete, and the competitors were genuine heroes.

Young's event would require the cars to be built before 1960, an era when cars were still simple to work on and of limited performance. The magical 80-days figure echoed the travels of Philias Phogg, Jules Verne's globe-circling character from the 1879 novel. At that early stage, the route was sketchy but would differ dramatically from the 1908 race. Young proposed traveling east from London, across central Europe and the former Soviet Union, across China and then North America. From there the original plan called for a Trans-Atlantic cruise to return competitors to a triumphant finish in London. Strangely, although Young had borrowed heavily from the symbolism of the 1907 event for his 1997 Peking to Paris run, he made almost no reference to the 1908 New York to Paris race in describing the Around the World Challenge. Was it possible that he didn't consider a success by Schuster's American team, driving an American-built car, to be noteworthy? In any case, I had gone looking for adventure and had found it. I sent in a deposit to hold my spot in the entry list. But how would I ever make the whole thing happen?

To start, I called Christopher Jensen at the *Cleveland Plain Dealer*.

George Schuster (behind steering wheel) was the lead driver of the American Thomas Flyer in the 1908 Nerw York to Paris race. *Courtesy of the Detroit Public Library, National Automotive History Collection*

Jensen had participated in more epic long-distance motoring events than anyone in America. His typical modus operandi was to borrow a brand-new vehicle from an automobile manufacturer and then convince the event organizers to let him follow the entire route as a journalist. In this way Chris, often accompanied by his wife, Cheryl, had participated in events all over the globe. Several years prior he had participated in the Paris-Moscow-Beijing Rally that covered much of the same ground that I would be driving through in what was then the Soviet Union and China. If anyone would know the lay of the land, I figured it would be Chris.

When I called, he was just preparing to leave for Nick Brittan's "Shield of Africa" rally, where he and Cheryl would report on the competition while driving a new Jeep Grand Cherokee.

Chris was immediately envious about my plans but doubtful that anyone could pull off an event of almost three months' duration. He suggested I cover the event as a journalist in a modern vehicle to avoid the pitfalls and potential mechanical mayhem of running in an old car. But I wanted to *compete* in the event as well as cover it, which meant I would need to drive a classic car. We finally agreed that the two most important factors would be the choice of a car and the choice of a co-driver. I asked Chris outright if he would like to join me, but with his upcoming event and work schedule, he said there would be no way for him to leave his real job for three months. I set about searching for a car and sponsors while Chris promised to help me find a co-driver who could share the adventure just as soon as he returned from Africa.

2

Mighty Mercedes

Is such a journey possible? Theoretically it is, but it must be borne in mind that the motor car, after woman, is the most fragile and capricious thing on earth.
— *Daily Mail of London*, 1908

It never occurred to us to do the event in anything but the Talbot. It's the car we do events with.
— Carrie Balfour, Car #15,
1933 Talbot AV 105

Few car collectors in America drive their cars more than a thousand miles a year. For many, a classic car is a pleasant conveyance for a sunny Sunday afternoon drive, but the thought of a long trip in an old car is inconceivable. For the Around the World event proposed by the Classic Rally Association, we would be driving more than 21,000 miles in cars built before 1960. Could this even be done? In countries around the globe potential entrants scratched their heads and dug through old books and back issues of magazines trying to find a car that would survive the rigors of the journey. Some looked no further than their own garages, convinced that one of the classic cars they already owned would be the best possible choice.

My own garage just happened to hold a car that might work for the event. A year earlier I had begun rebuilding a 1927 Chrysler Model 70 Roadster in the style of the Chryslers that had successfully run in the 24 Hours of LeMans in 1928 and 1929. These large six-cylinder cars were ahead of their time; they had hydraulic four-wheel brakes and advanced suspensions. My car had been modified with lightweight racing fenders and skimpy running boards which would make it a great choice for a long distance rough-and-tumble adventure. The engine had just been rebuilt and was ready to go back into the chassis, and the car had recently returned from the paint shop with a white body and black fenders. Closing my eyes, I could easily imagine roaring across some faraway desert in this towering and formidable beast.

There was a problem with this plan, however. Young announced that the entry fee for his Around the World Motor Challenge would be a cool $77,000 U.S. dollars. For me to raise this kind of money from sponsors would be nearly impossible without a significant contribution from an automobile manufacturer. Fortunately, my primary employer, *Automobile Magazine*, had strong ties with Chrysler Corporation, and I set about trying to exploit that relationship.

Chrysler Corporation was the public relations darling of the 1990s. Under the able leadership of Public Relations head Steve Harris and Tom Kowaleski, the company pulled off media stunts that rivaled Roman circuses. Chrysler also saw value in its own history and began sponsoring classic car tour events like the annual California Mille event for rich West coast auto enthusiasts, and the Perfect Ten Tour old car event circumnavigating Lake Michigan that *Automobile Magazine* had created a year earlier. What's more, corporate higher-ups like Bob Lutz and Francois Castaing were openly enthusiastic about old cars, and these executives each owned several interesting examples. Chrysler would seem to be the perfect company to sponsor my 1920s roadster on this adventure.

My timing was, unfortunately, off by about a year. Chrysler Corporation had reorganized; Lutz was now part of Chrysler history. Castaing was on his way out, too. New people were in charge of marketing and advertising, and the Public Relations staff was hobbled. Still, there was a chance they might do something, so I sent a letter with a proposal and hoped for the best. It was a bad sign when I called Chrysler two weeks later and nobody remembered seeing my proposal or letter. I put together another package and sent it to an advertising manager at Chrysler. Another week went by, and another phone call told me even more. He hadn't read the proposal yet and wanted me to call him back in a week. I began to collect the phone numbers of contacts at other car companies. A couple of weeks later, when I finally was able to get through to the ad manager, he told me that he couldn't see any value in sponsoring a 1920s Chrysler roadster, driven by an automotive journalist in the first-ever automobile rally around the world. Chrysler's concept of value had changed.

I refocused on what kind of car I would want to drive over such a long distance. It would need to be rugged and reliable. It also needed to have enough space to carry spares, tools, food and clothing for two people for three months. It should also, at least in my mind, have a bit of style. The romance of an open pre–War car still appealed to me. At first glance this would seem a poor choice as pre–War cars are typically slow and crude with marginal braking systems and few creature comforts. On the other side of the ledger, they were designed to drive on rough unmade roads and are robust in their construction. Pre-War cars are also quite simple in design with no complicated electronics to fail. The few rules that had been released at this point by the organizers hinted that pre–War cars would have their own special classification and would benefit from longer time allowances for each day's drive. The problem was, the companies that built many of the high quality pre–War cars like Packard and Pierce Arrow aren't around any more, so the chances of successfully hitting up a manufacturer for sponsorship seemed slim.

In many ways, it had been easier for George Schuster in 1908. He worked for the Thomas Company of Buffalo New York; they simply told him one day to pack his bags and provided him with a new 1907 Thomas Flyer. It was a good and fast car and one that the Thomas factory test driver knew very well.

"The $4,000 Thomas Flyer of 1907 was a proven machine, one of the greatest cars of its day. It had a 4-cylinder, 60-horsepower engine, and each had to climb Buffalo's Brewery Hill in high gear and do 55 to 60 miles an hour in a road test, before being delivered to a customer," recalled Schuster, nearly 60 years later.

Yes, the Thomas was a splendid choice in 1908, but it didn't solve my problem as the Thomas Company had gone out of business in 1912.

I sent letters to Public Relations heads at all of the American car companies. Buick had sponsored two cars in the Peking to Paris Rally in 1997 and so seemed a possibility. I spoke with Larry Gustin at Buick a week after sending him my letter. Pre-War Buicks were well respected for their quality and toughness and would make a good choice. Larry was interested in doing something, but was unable to commit to any specific sponsorship amount. He suggested I contact Pat and Mary Brooks, two Americans from Iowa whom Buick had supported in the Peking event and who were also planning on driving around the world. I figured they probably were in the same boat as me — looking for sponsorship money — and I didn't see where we could help each other. So I pressed on, contacting public relations and marketing people at a dozen different car companies. I was disappointed as it was becoming increasingly clear that the interest in a pre–War car was minimal. For some reason I seemed unable to get the marketing experts to share my romantic view of running boards, flowing fenders and the roaring twenties. I shifted my focus to cars made in the 1950s. This line of thought led me to Volkswagen. The retrospectively styled New Beetle had just been introduced and was named Automobile of the Year by our magazine. What's more, an air-cooled Bug from the fifties would be easy to repair in the field and would benefit from the lack of a vulnerable water radiator. These cars had been highly successful in races in the rough Australian outback throughout the 1950s, and lots of knowledge from Baja races in Mexico had also been gained since then. In many ways, a VW Beetle suddenly seemed my perfect choice. I gave VW my full attention, but after several fruitless weeks of telephone calls, a Volkswagen spokesman finally told me, "Volkswagen isn't really interested in promoting its history." I looked at the New Beetle with its clearly retro shape and shook my head once again. Was I the only person getting it?

I hit the history books again to look for a car that was a success as a rally car from a company that was still in existence. Volvo, Saab, Porsche and Ford were all subjected to my scrutiny. Then I found it. Mercedes-Benz had a long and illustrious competition history. The pre–War Grand Prix cars were all-conquering, as were the company's racing cars and 300SL sports car in the fifties. I thought a 300SL Gullwing Mercedes would be a wonderful choice. In 1955, Belgian driver Olivier Gendebien won the incredibly tough Liege-Rome-Liege rally in a privately entered 300SL. The factory driver Walter Schock used one to win the rough Acropolis Rally in Greece in 1956. The 300SL is powerful, fast and extremely glamorous. For a brief instant I imagined my elegantly attired self pulling up to the portico of a French Chateau for cocktails at the end of a day's rally run. That fantasy vanished in an instant with the reality that the cheapest 300SL available would cost well over $150,000, ten times more than my theoretical car budget could withstand. On the more humble end of the scale, Mercedes-Benz did rally its sedans during the 1950s and early 1960s with good success.

Mercedes-Benz sedans were quite advanced in the 1950s. The largest was the 220 series with four doors, a six-cylinder engine, four-speed manual transmission and independent front and rear suspension that would smooth out the bumps and potholes we would encounter on our drive around the world. The cars had run a number of rallies in Europe and Walter Schock had even finished second on the prestigious Monte Carlo Rally in 1956. A quick check of the classifieds showed prices of these often overlooked classics to be between $4,000 and $8,000, depending upon condition. What's more, my hero Innes Ireland from *Sideways to Sydney* had driven a privately entered Mercedes in his big adventure. As he had written about his own choice of vehicles, "Reliability and toughness would be the qualities that ensured the car would be capable of making the journey, but allied to this, it would have to provide a high degree of crew comfort as well as a good turn of speed." So just as it had been for Innes Ireland on the London to Sydney rally in 1968, Mercedes-Benz was a possibility, but would they want to play?

This time, instead of just sending a letter I made a phone call. Stephen

Rossi was then the General Manager of Corporate Communications at Mercedes-Benz of North America, Inc. I had known Steve since the days he held a similar position at Saab. Rossi is a bright and imaginative collector of old cars and motorcycles. He is a real car guy, and if anyone would understand the value of this adventure, it would be Steve Rossi. I reached him at his New Jersey office and quickly outlined what I had in mind and how I would make it happen. Rossi was immediately enthusiastic.

"I'm not sure exactly how we'll be involved," Rossi said, "But count us in!" I promised to send him a full package with all of the details and hung up with my heart soaring. For the first time in the three months since committing to the adventure, I suddenly had hope that I might be able to pull it off.

I put together a creative proposal for Mercedes-Benz that included an outline of what car I would use, what I knew about the proposed route, the kind of coverage Mercedes could expect and a timeline of when everything would happen. My friend Larry Crane, who was at that time Art Director at *Automobile Magazine*, graced my proposal with his original artwork. Larry drew a sketch of a 1950s Mercedes-Benz sedan careening around a

Larry Crane produced this concept of what my Mercedes-Benz 220S would look like on the event. *Larry Crane*

corner past the mosques and minarets of the Middle East. I would end up using this drawing on all of my subsequent pleas for sponsorship, and to this day the original drawing is framed and holds a place of honor on my office wall. I was asking Mercedes to cover approximately half of the $77,000 entry fee and to help out with parts for the car that I would be preparing for the adventure. (Mercedes-Benz is one of the few companies that still make and stock original replacement parts for their earlier models.) It took less than a week for Mercedes-Benz to say yes to my proposal, and I was in business. In business? Hell, I was dancing in the aisles.

Next, I would need to find a car. The car I was looking for needed to have a solid chassis and body. I would be rebuilding the engine and running gear, as well as modifying the suspension, so none of these items needed to be in first-class condition. Likewise, the interior would be largely gutted to hold two rally-style seats, a rollover bar and a large container for spare parts and equipment. I scoured the want ads and eventually found exactly what I was looking for in *The Star*, the publication of the Mercedes-Benz Club of America. The car was a 1959 Mercedes-Benz 220S Sedan. Although less powerful than the 220SE version with its mechanical fuel injection, the twin carburetor-equipped 220S car promised to be easier to repair in the field, should anything go wrong. The car had around 140,000 miles on it, which was not too bad, considering that everything would even-

My vintage 1959 Mercedes follows a new Mercedes-Benz M-Class home.

tually be rebuilt or replaced. I called the owner in West Virginia and arranged to come to see the car, promising to bring along a trailer in case I decided the car was the right one for me.

The drive from Michigan to West Virginia was made easier by the loan of a new M-Class Mercedes-Benz sport utility vehicle. I borrowed it from the Mercedes press fleet to get some experience in the towing capability of this vehicle. The fact that I was going to pick up an old Mercedes-Benz with a brand new one and that this would be a good photo opportunity wasn't lost on me. When I got to West Virginia, the old car was everything it was promised to be. The elderly couple had owned it forever and only used it on weekends to drive into town for dinner at a local restaurant. It was gleaming black and reasonably solid with only a small amount of underside rust. The engine was tired and smoky, but it ran. After a brief test drive, I gave the owner $4,300 and loaded the car onto the trailer behind the new Mercedes-Benz ML320. Driving home, the taillights of the tow vehicle cast a rosy reflection onto the chrome grille and headlights of the old car on the trailer. I realized that the thousand-mile round trip that I was driving to pick up the car was less than five percent of the more than twenty thousand miles I would be driving once the rally started. Still, I now had a car to drive around the world.

While all of the car dealings were taking place, I was also concerned about finding the right co-driver for this adventure. It's been said that a rally co-driver needs to be as agile as a cat, as strong as a gorilla, as brave as Dick Tracy and able to compute square roots in an earthquake. That described the person I was looking for. At one point in my life I had been involved with professional rallying in this country. Pro-rallying, as practiced in the U.S., is about as invisible as any professional sport can be. Cars are sent out one at a time over rough dirt and gravel roads. The roads are closed to other traffic, and the shortest time taken over each of the closed sections wins. It is just about the most exciting kind of racing a person can do, but as it is difficult to televise it has almost no following in America. In Europe and Asia, however, rallying is huge, approaching soccer in its fan appeal. With my background in this obscure sport, I at least knew whom to ask about finding a co-driver. One thing was certain: I did not want to bring one of my best friends on this rally. Three months in a car will surely test any relationship. I felt if I found a professional, someone with whom I had no previous ties, I'd be better off. If at the end of our adventure my co-driver and I remained friends, great. But if we hated each other after 80 days of pressure, living in a cramped car, at least I wouldn't have lost a friend.

Meanwhile, Chris Jensen and his wife, Cheryl, had returned from the rally in Africa. It had been harrowing, especially in the southern part of the

Top: The imposing front grille of a 1959 Mercedes-Benz 220S sedan. *Bottom:* Interior condition wasn't important, as we knew we would be using competition seats.

continent when the event was entangled in the suppression of a civil upris-
ing. Chris and Cheryl had just managed to slip past a smoldering border
station after it had been decimated by a helicopter gunship. It made me
appreciate all the more how important the person sitting next to me for three
months would be.

I made some inquiries, and one name kept coming to the surface: Mark
Rinkel, a dentist who lived in Hinckley, Ohio, a suburb of Cleveland. In
addition to competing in the pro-rally series as a co-driver in a Ford Escort,
Mark had recently run Nick Brittan's Panama to Alaska Rally driving in the
touring class in a massive Chevrolet Suburban. In fact, while looking for a
journalist to cover his exploits in that event, Rinkel had actually contacted
me, asking if I would like to ride along on part of the trip to Alaska. Chris
Jensen also knew Mark and said positive things about him. I sent Mark an
e-mail, letting him know that I was putting together an entry for the around
the world event and that the co-driver seat was still open.

Mark's response was interested but guarded. So many would-be adventurers talk about doing big events without ever actually doing the hard work
to make things happen. I get offers all the time to join a team or become
part of a group that promises to do something truly epic. These promises
rarely amount to anything, so I understood Rinkel's hesitation. Besides, I
hadn't really offered him anything; I had just mentioned that I would be
putting together a team to compete in an event that was still two years away.
If Mark had jumped in with both feet without checking things out, I would
have been suspicious.

Meanwhile in London, Philip Young was scheduling a get-together for
competitors who had run his Peking to Paris event six months earlier. He
also was promising to use the opportunity as a get-acquainted party for
teams that were interested in competing in his Around the World event. I
wanted to meet Young as well as talk to some of the other competitors. If
I was going to commit more than two years of my life, three months of
travel, a whole pile of money and my reputation as an automotive writer
to this thing, I wanted to meet the guy in charge. I booked a ticket from
Detroit to London and contacted Young in his London office. I pleaded that
as a working journalist he might consider helping me out with my hotel
room for my visit. To my surprise, he agreed to book me a room in Kens-
ington, not far from the Royal Geographical Society where the meeting
would take place.

In the map room of the Royal Geographical Society in London there's
a framed portrait of Stanley. On the opposite wall hangs a portrait of Livingstone. Yes, *that* Stanley and *that* Livingstone. Explorers, adventurers,
charlatans, scoundrels and heroes had all trod the worn hardwood floors
where I now stood. The hall was the same Main Lecture Theater in which

Captain Scott had spoken of his remarkable deeds in the Antarctic before his fatal trip to the South Pole. You had to hand it to Philip Young; he understood the value of history.

At the get-together there were two groups: those who had run the grueling Peking to Paris, their bronze, silver or gold finishers medals pinned to their evening clothes, their eyes gazing far away as though still transfixed by the sights they had seen; and the rest of us, mere mortals and wannabes who were here to find out more, to find out if it was really possible. Conversations always came back to the main theme: "Fuel consumption will be critical...." "Of course that's a very good car, but not really up to this sort of terrain..." "80 days, almost three months in a car, my god..."

The map of the route was spellbinding. Imagine leaving London's famous Tower Bridge, traveling across Europe and crossing the Caspian Sea. Then to the fabled Silk Route, visiting the mosques of Samarkand. Then into China crossing the Taklamakan Desert. Loosely translated, Taklamakan means "you may go in, but you will never come out." If we got out, we would push on to Beijing and an airlift to Anchorage. But that would only be half of the adventure as the Alaskan and Canadian wilderness and the back roads of rural America would still need to be traversed.

At this early stage in the planning, Phillip Young wanted to put all of the cars on a ship and cruise across the Atlantic, returning to London's Tower Bridge. That plan would eventually change to another airlift, this time to Marrakech. But at the moment, standing on the same hallowed ground as Scott and Shackleton had trod, it all seemed so exotic, so exciting. Young, wisely understanding that not everyone can take off work for a solid 80 days, had decided to make the first part of the trip, from London to Beijing, its own separate event. There would only be space for 40 cars to be airlifted from Beijing to Anchorage and to continue around the world. Miss the plane from Beijing, and you would be out for good and possibly stranded in China.

At the party I met the Englishman Phil Surtees who had won the 1997 Peking to Paris rally in a 1942 Willys Army Jeep. Old and crusty, Surtees had lost a couple of fingers when his Jeep had rolled over on him while practicing before he had even set out on the Peking to Paris challenge. He was less than complimentary about the level of preparation his fellow competitors had lavished on their cars on that event. He also had little good to say about Philip Young.

I also spoke with American Linda Dodwell, who, with journalist Genny Obert, had won the Women's Prize in a sixties British Hillman sedan. Dodwell said she really didn't enjoy the time she had spent driving her car from Peking to Paris. "I can't imagine wanting to sit in a car all the way around the world," she admitted to me, and I understood why she wouldn't be going along. Dodwell had bankrolled the trip with Obert, who was a California automotive journalist and a colleague of mine at *European Car* magazine. Genny had written a fine book, *Prince Borghese's Trail* (Council Oak Books), detailing her and Linda's run in a 1960s Hillman Hunter. I knew that Genny Obert wanted to do the Around the World event, but with Dodwell uninterested, Genny wasn't having much luck lining anything up.

Philip Young was the person I had really come to meet. He was a large man, standing just a bit shorter than my six foot two inch height. He must have weighed well over 250 pounds, and looked to be in his mid-forties. His youthful face was crowned by a shock of black hair that he wore parted to one side. He seemed ill at ease talking to people one-to-one and had a brusque manner that bordered on rude. Okay, sometimes it overran that border. Even when speaking directly to you, Young seemed to be a thousand miles away, driving up a rally road in some unpronounceable part of the world. His character underwent a remarkable transformation when he stood before a microphone. Suddenly he was warm and engaging, managing the masses and smoothly delivering both good and bad news. It's almost as if he saved all of his personality for those moments when he spoke before a crowd. I didn't find him pleasant company; but I was convinced that if on the event I needed to be rescued from a Chinese prison, Philip Young would be someone who could do it. Even though it was getting harder and harder to find anyone at the meeting who would say something nice about him, I was more convinced than ever that I would have to be a part of this enormous adventure.

I returned from London and sent Mark an invitation to join my team. He readily agreed, and with the Mercedes-Benz commitment officially in place, we gave ourselves the name "U.S. Mercedes Team." With a little less than two years to go, it seemed to me that there would be plenty of time to get ready. I was wrong.

3

Get Ready, Get Set...

"We put blocks on top of the axles to give more road clearance and added a 35-gallon gasoline tank. Especially heavy radius rods had been machined and were installed. The car had been equipped with metal fenders; these were removed, and in their place, aprons of heavy leather were attached. An oil reservoir had been carried on the running board. This was relocated so that gravity would act. Every-where the spirit of the race had entered into the men of the factory, and they labored throughout the night and part of the next day to put the car into condition."
— George Schuster with Tom Mahoney, *The Longest Auto Race, New York to Paris 1908*, Copyright 1966.

Having a car and a co-driver was a good start, but before the rally began on May 1st, 2000, I would need to have a lot more working capital. Only half of the entry fee had been covered by my new benefactors at Mercedes-Benz, and the additional costs of airlifts, airline tickets, hotels and car preparation would eat up another $40,000–$50,000. On the plus side, we were designated as the official team of Mercedes-Benz in North America, and I planned to leverage this as much as I could in my search for more sponsors. Bridgestone Tire came on board soon after. The company not only promised to provide us with its Dueler light truck tires, but also provided the other half of the entry fee. The light truck tires were a good choice, as we needed their strength on rough rock strewn roads and the grip of an aggressive tread pattern when traversing through mud holes.

Mark convinced Llumar, one of his sponsors from Panama to Alaska to kick in some money. This Virginia-based company makes window-tinting films. I couldn't see why we would want this done to our car but was later surprised by how well the tinting worked to cut glare and heat, especially when crossing fearsome deserts. Other automotive companies like Bosch, Mobil, PPG Industries and TechSight (an automotive-oriented division of defense contractor General Dynamics) would eventually come on board with financial and product support, while others like Bilstein, Eibach Springs, Nikon, and NutriBiotics would supply their products for us to use on the adventure.

Meanwhile, back in England, Philip Young was adjusting the rules. Unable to find enough entrants with cars built before 1960, he suddenly upped the cutoff date to cars built before 1968. This was a big change. Car technology had progressed a lot in those eight years. Instead of drum brakes and carburetors, many cars built in the late 1960s had much more effective disc brakes. Some even had sophisticated fuel injection systems that would compensate for altitude and poor fuel much more efficiently than old-fashioned carburetors could. Suspension systems had improved, as had basic creature comforts inside the car. To compensate a bit, Young would now accept changing to front disc brakes and alternators on the older cars. Nevertheless, the rule changes meant instead of rumbling across the terrain at a sedate 40-mph, the leading cars would be capable of hammering along at much higher speeds. The advantage of a faster car is that you get to each day's finish several hours earlier than those who are at the rear of the pack in a slower vehicle. The extra time can be used for repairs or a few more hours of sleep, both important on an event that would last three months. Going faster also means a lot more wear and tear on the car and a different kind of event than the pure endurance test I had initially expected. I suspended all work on our 1959 Mercedes-Benz and began looking for a suitable later car built by the German company.

Mercedes-Benz was quite prolific during the sixties. In addition to a range of six-cylinder sedan models, the company also built three versions of a two-seat sports car. The 230SL was introduced in 1963. It was fast and light when compared to the company's sedans and even gained a rally history when Eugen Bohringer used one to win the 1963 Spa-Sofia-Liege Rally. Through 1968, the engine size increased as the car was renamed 250SL and 280SL. I looked carefully at this model, trying to imagine two oversized American males cooped up in the cramped two-seat cockpit for eighty days. Where would our spare parts and tools fit? As appealing as the SL sports car might be, it just wouldn't work for us.

Mercedes had built another great sporting car. In 1965, the company announced its 250 SE Coupe. Based upon the stylish 220 Coupe, this car was fitted with a larger and much more powerful engine. It had an attractive two-door body and was quite advanced with four-wheel disc brakes and a fuel-injected engine. This was a large car in which Mark and I could comfortably keep our distance. I began searching the national want ads and quickly found a 1967 250 SE Coupe in Texas, not far from Dallas. At $8,000,

Top: This 1967 Mercedes-Benz 250SE was nearly our ride around the world. *Bottom:* We were talked out of this stylish and comfortable car by event organizer Philip Young.

the price was reasonable as the engine had been recently rebuilt and had received several upgrades in the process. Besides, what was another $8,000? I felt like a traitor to the car I had already started working on but it didn't stop me from putting together a cashier's check, jumping onto an airplane and landing on a Thursday morning at the Dallas airport.

The owner was waiting for me at the curbside. He had driven the car to the airport, followed by his wife in another car. The car looked good. It was painted a metallic brown with brown seats and interior. Not my first choice perhaps, but at least it wouldn't show dirt. There were a few stone chips and light scratches, but the car was quite presentable. I opened the hood and saw that all looked in order. I signed over the check as he signed the title, and I began a 600-mile drive from Texas back to Michigan.

Most people would consider it insane to drive a 30-year old car 600 miles after buying it sight-unseen. But I have made several such trips in old cars and have only had a few problems. Besides, my theory is, if you can get the car as close to home as possible, you can always rent a U-Haul truck and trailer to get it the rest of the way. The way I see it, finding solutions to problems on the road are excellent practice for long-distance endurance events. I'd driven to Michigan in an old short-wheelbase Land Rover from Maryland and in a vintage 1967 Ferrari 330GT from Phoenix in the middle of winter and the trips had taught me a lot about how to keep an old car going. The most important tool you can carry is a cellular telephone. If things go beyond your abilities to fix them, you can always call for help. Several credit cards are next on the list. There's almost nothing that can't be fixed with a credit card. Still, I like to bring a pair of pliers, a couple of assorted screwdrivers, duct tape and some strong wire along on any old-car trip. A small battery charger is also a good bet, with an extension cord so that you can shore up a balky electrical system with overnight charges. The truth is, you never seem to have exactly what you need, and you learn to make do with what you can find along the way.

Fortunately, such dramatics were completely unnecessary, as the Mercedes Coupe made the 12-hour trip from Texas with complete reliability. It was fast and comfortable, cruising along the interstate highways at an easy 70 mph. Best of all, I really liked it. When I got home, I faxed a letter to Philip Young to inform him we would be changing cars to the newer and more competitive 1968 250SE Coupe.

What I didn't expect was the response I received. He was at the same time negative about our change and dismissive about the car's chances of finishing the event. While admitting that there would be several similar newer cars competing in the event, Young said that these would be touring entries with little or no chance of doing well in the standings. His fax, with its implication of the severity of the roads, was disturbing.

With so little time remaining, we needed to start work preparing one of the two Mercedes-Benz cars I now owned. The 1968 Coupe was truly a beauty and would be a luxurious way to travel around the world. It was also fast, with significantly more power and performance than the 1959 sedan. I really enjoyed driving it and had no trouble imagining myself sitting on the starting line in London in this ever-so-stylish 1960's coupe. But Philip Young was telling us its superior performance wouldn't matter, that the test would be one of endurance and not speed. My Mercedes-Benz sponsors were happy with either car and left the choice to me. What to do? I put each car on a lift and looked at them from the underside. The sedan was built like a tank. Everything was massively constructed and well protected. The coupe, being a Mercedes, was also strongly built, just not quite up to the rugged standards of the sedan.

I had to make a decision. Although the Coupe's style and performance was seductive, my final choice was to stay with the somewhat frumpy 1959 220S sedan. It had a certain honesty and puppy-dog charm that was matched by its rugged durability. I liked the car but just hoped I had made the right decision in choosing it over the coupe. I found a buyer for my now-spurned Coupe and was truly sorry to see it go.

Now that I knew what kind of car I would drive, I needed a recipe to build it into a rally car. This is a bit like baking a cake in that you need to find all the right ingredients and then put them together in the right order. Because Mercedes-Benz cars were so successful on rough rallies in the past that it seemed rational that the recipe the factory used would make a good starting point. I began talking to as many people as I could find about the strengths and weaknesses of the car and how to make improvements. It seemed like everyone I talked to had an opinion, many of which were in direct opposition to someone else's.

Then I found Don Blackburn. Don lives in California and had run a 1958 Mercedes 220SE Coupe in the La Carrera Mexican road race with great success. This is an all-out six-day race across the rough roads of Mexico. If a car can survive La Carrera, it has a pretty good chance of doing well anywhere. It turned out that Don's car was well prepared and successful and underwent many of the same modifications I would want to make on my car. Don also had about 40 pages of the original specifications from the factory for rally cars of the 1950s and early 60s. He was more than willing to share what he knew with me. That was indeed helpful, but even more useful was the advice he gave me to not believe or trust anything that anybody said about how to make an old Mercedes-Benz into a rally car. "Just follow to the letter what the factory did with their cars," said Blackburn. He knew what he was talking about, having learned from experience that few people really knew anything of value about preparing and manhandling one of these old German beasts.

Work progresses on our dumpy Mercedes sedan.

With most of the recipe in hand, I could go about collecting the ingredients. Running an old Mercedes-Benz gave me several important secret weapons. The cars were, of course, immensely strong and well built, but they also progressed in their technology from year to year and vehicle to vehicle. This meant that the front disc brakes that were introduced by Mercedes-Benz in 1963 would bolt directly onto my earlier 1959 model. It also meant that I could replace the awkward column change gear shifter with a four-speed floor change transmission from a later car. I rationalized that I was used to driving a stick shift with its shifter on the floor. Trying to find a gear with the column shifter in an emergency might be a problem.

I also anticipated that the compression ratio of the engine, while fine for everyday driving in civilized places in the U.S. and Europe, would be too high for the wilds of China and the countries of the former Soviet Union where the organizers had warned anyone that would listen that we should expect low 70-octane gasoline. Low octane gasoline requires a low engine compression ratio, or the result is engine failure from melted pistons. Once again, the parts interchangeability of various years of Mercedes model's parts helped out. I was able to find a used cylinder head in Texas from a 1957 Mercedes-Benz sedan with a compression ratio several points lower

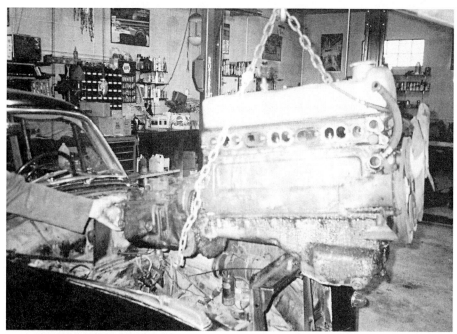

Top: Welded rear suspension bracing would help us on rough roads. *Bottom:* Pulling the engine and transmission so that they could be rebuilt.

than the original one in my car. I had it shipped then rebuilt it with all new parts in the valve train.

Perhaps the most important factor in our car preparation was the immense support that Mercedes-Benz maintains for its older cars. Nearly every part for my forty year old Mercedes was readily available from the factory. None of the parts I needed for rebuilding the car would be cheap imitations. All were factory original Mercedes-Benz parts made to the same original quality standards. As I began to disassemble my old sedan, the list of parts to replace and repair began to grow. The engine went to an Ann Arbor machine shop for a full rebuild, and I began scouring junkyards and private caches of Mercedes-Benz parts to get the things I needed.

After Philip Young's note about car choice and rough roads, the biggest concern on the tough roads we anticipated was the tires. They needed to be capable of withstanding hour after hour of pounding and abuse at speeds that range from a crawl to more than 70 mph. Because of a need to keep the weight of the car low, I wanted to carry only two spare wheels and tires, which made the tire's durability the primary concern. Bridgestone's support would be a key factor here. Although known in motorsports for its Formula One racing accomplishments, Bridgestone has also had great success worldwide with its rally tires. For a while I thought about using specialized rally competition tires for the event but worried that, while fast and rugged, they might wear out far too quickly. I knew that there would be no chance for re-supply for the month that we would be crossing China. Bridgestone also has an extensive selection of light truck and commercial tires that I was able to choose from, looking for durability instead of outright speed. The rules allowed me to increase wheel diameter by one inch over the stock size, so I chose two different 14-inch Bridgestone light truck tires to test once the car was completed. That would mean I would need 14-inch wheels to replace the 13-inch wheels that originally came with the car. Although alloy wheels would look nice, I knew that steel wheels would handle the punishment better and could be repaired easily, even in the wilds of China. Later model Mercedes-Benz sedans had come with 14-inch steel wheels, so it was back to the junkyards to find what I needed.

One of my chief concerns for the car was the heavy load it would need to carry. With driver, co-driver, 22 gallons of fuel, emergency drinking water, two spare wheels and tires, spare parts, tools, food and clothing, the 220S weighed in at two tons, about a thousand pounds more than its original weight. The extra load would put an un-modified car's suspension onto its bump stops and dramatically reduce its ground clearance. This problem was eventually solved with help from Eibach Springs. The forty-year-old German company, with facilities in California, provides springs for production cars like Ferraris and also has extensive experience in racing and rallying all over the world. Gary Peek, vice president of sales and marketing at Eibach, took an interest in my project and agreed to make me two sets of springs that would not only carry the load, but also raise the car slightly for even better ground clearance. The only problem was that my car was in Michigan, and the Eibach engineers were in California. Gary's solution was a detailed instruction sheet which told me exactly how to make the dozens of loaded and unloaded measurements the engineers would need. A long afternoon with a tape measure, some bags of cement and buckets of water for ballast, and the measurements were accomplished.

There was no doubt the suspension would take quite a pounding, and unless the shock absorbers were up to the job the car could become uncontrollable on a really rough road. Bilstein's gas shock absorbers are just the thing for these tough conditions, and the company agreed to provide us with two sets. The load and ride height were given to the company so that they could find the right shock for our extreme application. It ended up taking several tries to get the valving right, but in the end the shocks provided plenty of suspension control on rough roads.

After considerable soul searching, I decided that our Around the World Mercedes would need to have a roll bar and fuel cell. To Americans living in a world of lawsuits, it seemed a bit strange that the organizers required neither. We calculated that we needed to carry 22 gallons of gasoline to make the 320-mile range the organizers said would be required. The stock gas tank was 17.2 gallons and wouldn't do it. Although engineers work hard to make a car's fuel system safe, carrying extra fuel was going to be dangerous. The safest way I know to carry fuel is in an explosion-proof racing fuel cell. If a bus hit us in Istanbul, I didn't want to go out in a blaze of glory. By reconstructing the floor of the trunk, we were able to carry a 22-gallon fuel cell there and still have room for two spare tires, a hydraulic jack and miscellaneous spare parts and tow ropes. Mounting the fuel cell in the trunk, we got it away from rocks and road impacts. Twin electric fuel pumps and a special water trapping fuel filter made by Racor completed our system.

Building a roll cage for the car was a bigger decision. It would add weight, which was something we wanted to keep to a minimum, but if we were to come around a corner and find the road blocked by a truck, bus, or cow, we might need to take to a field or ditch in avoidance. The extra support of the roll bar would prevent the body shell from distorting and keep the windshield and rear window from breaking. Instead of a major problem and lengthy repairs, the car could be righted and continue on its way in a much shorter time. A full roll cage can be a dangerous thing if you drive in a car without wearing a helmet as your head can strike the cross bars in a really serious crash. We finally decided on a roll-over bar that would keep the body shell intact if the worst should happen, while also not being quite as heavy as a full roll-cage would have been. I found an excellent hot-rod fabricator in southern Michigan who not only built our roll-bar, but constructed additional braces to reinforce the rear shock absorber mounts. Another metal fabricator, Dave Boenke, added bracing to the front suspension A-arms, reconstructed the floor of the trunk to hold the fuel cell and two spare tires and added reinforcement welds to the steel wheels. I did everything I could think of to make the body and suspension as tough as possible.

Although most of our driving would take place in daylight, falling behind or stopping to make repairs would mean we would need to cover ground quickly over bad roads at night. Our insurance in this case came from auxiliary driving lights. Hella helped us here, and having used their lights in places like Alaska, Central America, and Europe, I knew they made a product that could be relied upon. The organizers of the rally, in an effort to make the cars look more period than modern, decreed that driving lights could be no larger than 7 inches in diameter. That was pretty small by today's rally light standards, but fortunately Hella made a range of driving and fog patterns in the Rallye 160 model, which complied with the size requirements.

Time sped by, and progress on the car was slow. I had created a detailed schedule with clear milestones to be met, but we seemed unable to adhere to the schedule. I was doing much of the work by myself, and there just weren't enough hours every week to work my regular job and build a car to drive around the world. Still, I was making progress. I would remove a part, the steering box or driveshaft for example, bring it to a specialist, and pick it up a week or two later, completely rebuilt and ready for installation. The pile of ready-to-install parts grew larger and larger.

As work progressed on the car, Mark and I decided we needed to work on building our team. We had never run a rally together. We remedied that situation in the beginning of 1999 by running the Ontario Winter Rally. I borrowed a Subaru Impreza RS press car and had Bridgestone ship us a set of Blizzak winter tires.

The rally took place far from civilization in Northern Canada in the middle of the night in the dead of winter. The roads were ice- and snow-covered and slippery as thirty cars left the start. The all-wheel drive Subaru was excellent in these conditions. I began to knock the rust off of my rally driving skills and was delighted to find that my instincts were quick to return. Even with the handicap of only having stock headlights, we stayed in the top three through the first two sections, eventually falling to sixth overall when I started getting too careful with my borrowed car. Mark and I discovered we were both competitive by nature and each of us could do the job we signed on for. But could we do it for three straight months?

Mark and I competed with this borrowed Subaru in the Ontario Winter Rally as a way to build our team.

With a year to go before the start, everything was progressing, but at times the irregularity of cash flow became discouraging. I was having reasonable success finding sponsors, but all of the money they sent us would immediately be turned over to the organizers to cover the next installment of the entry fee. Then, unexpectedly, Mark came up with a solution. He proposed that he purchase the rally car for an amount equal to what it would be worth when it was completed and ready to drive in the event. The money would be used to finish the car and pay the remaining bills, and in exchange he would own the car when the event was finished. For a brief instant I thought how much it would mean to me to own the car I had driven around the world, but I agreed to Mark's terms. He would be the owner of the rally car. It was an enormous help, and I appreciated the risk that Mark was taking. Mark later admitted to me that it was a kind of insurance policy for him. He was pretty sure I couldn't throw him off the team if he owned the car.

Time pressed forward. Originally, Mark and I had planned to run the Mercedes in several old car events as a shakedown. We figured on getting several thousand miles on the car to find out what worked and what didn't. Events we hoped to compete in with our car as a warm-up passed by with the car unfinished. After spending months working out of a warehouse filled with old cars in Ypsilanti, Michigan, we had moved the car to Mark's garage behind his home in Hinckley, Ohio, for its final assembly. My trips to Mark's house from Michigan were a good opportunity for us to learn to work together and figure out what made each other tick. Although Mark claimed no mechanical abilities, he was a good worker who was more than willing to work on the biggest parts and the smallest details. He decided that the car would need a better paint job than the cheap re-spray in original black that I had done in Michigan and arranged for the local Chevrolet dealership to repaint the car in a decidedly non-original bright white. On most of the sessions at Mark's house we would end up working late into the night, reassembling the suspension parts and designing skid-plates and exhaust pipe extensions that would help us over the toughest roads. It was good for team building, and we also reasoned that by working on the car ourselves, there wasn't much we wouldn't be able to fix on the road. Most competitors were rich enough to have someone else prepare their car, but we hoped our superior knowledge would give us an advantage somewhere down the line. Besides, with the outrageously high entry fee that Philip Young had set we couldn't afford to have someone else do the work. By midsummer we began planning a trip to England to attend Philip Young's driver's briefing at the old historic racetrack at Brooklands at the end of August.

Mark had traveled to Europe only once before. He flew into Gatwick airport and took the necessary trains to find his way to join me at The Ship Hotel in Weybridge, Surry, not far from the Brooklands circuit. His reputation as a top navigator was obviously well deserved. Several other rally teams were staying at the same hotel before the meeting, and we soon struck up a friendship with Ed and Beverly Suhrbier from California. Ed was a retired real estate developer, and he and his wife, Beverly, were entered in the London to Beijing leg of the rally in a 1957 Mercedes-Benz Cabriolet. Over a Thai dinner the night before the driver's briefing, Mark and I talked with Ed and Bev about the rally. It was clear from the questions they asked and the looks on their faces that our new friends from California hadn't considered that the event might be as tough as we were anticipating it to be. It was also clear from the look on his face that Mark didn't care for Thai food.

Several teams brought their rally cars to the Brooklands meeting. Mark and I were jealous. Our car hadn't moved under its own power in more than a year and still wouldn't be going anywhere for a month or more. We crawled over, around, and under each of the cars that were present, trying to learn something we had forgotten in the preparation of our own car. Then we all entered a huge meeting room to hear Philip Young and his group of experts and organizers tell us what we could expect on the event itself. Looking to the right and left, it was like the first day of summer camp, only the campers were all grown up and successful adults.

The first thing we learned was that we would need to have map books, and that they would cost $500. It's hard to imagine how you could put on a rally with a route book that provides the specific instructions to tell competitors where to go and how to get there, and then turn around and charge them for a set of the necessary maps, but there you are. Next, we learned that a special service to obtain travel visas would be available for a fifty-percent surcharge over the usual visa rates. Because you don't want to be caught going into Azerbaijan with the wrong papers, there wasn't much choice but to pay. Then came the heaviest hit. The two airlifts would cost 5,000 pounds sterling. Each. That meant an additional $16,000 would need to be paid to fly the cars from Beijing to Anchorage and from Newark to Marrakech. A package of hotel rooms (which was mandatory) would be another $8,000. Some reached for their checkbooks. Others nodded their heads in resignation. I panicked quietly at my seat. Beverly Suhrbier later told me the look of absolute despair on my face on hearing the news was almost painful to see. The entry costs to be paid to the organizers now totaled more than $100,000. I knew we would need to find more sponsors. Where would we ever find another $15,000–$20,000 less than eight months before the start of the rally? Every penny we had raised had already gone straight to Philip Young. And now he wanted even more.

Not that all of the meeting was bad financial news. We learned how the route would carry us across the former Soviet Union and China. We were told which immunization shots were recommended. (There were a lot of them.) We heard again that fuel in China was poor and that we would need low compression engines with effective water separation filters if we were to make it through. All the while, Philip Young remained aloof and unapproachable — his trademark. Mark and I made an appointment to see the taciturn Mr. Young the next day for lunch before we flew back to the States. I wanted to ask him some more questions, and also interview him for one of the many stories I had lined up about the event. That evening we had dinner again with the Suhrbiers. I was in a foul mood, desperate over the financial crisis that I knew was facing our team. It was inconceivable to me that Philip Young could announce an increase in costs of more than $20,000, and even more inconceivable that the entrants would accept this so readily. I was ready to ask Mr. Young some very serious questions.

The next day, the time for our meeting came and went with Mark and me waiting at our hotel with no sign of Philip Young. I finally reached him by phone in his office and discovered that he had forgotten about our meeting. I talked to him for twenty minutes on the phone, but he was dismissive of my concerns and clearly didn't wish to talk to me. I was beginning to understand why it was so difficult to find anyone who had anything good to say about Philip Young.

After returning from England, Mark and I redoubled our efforts, both on the car and on the search for more sponsorship money. Mark delighted in fabricating new parts and brackets, and as it turned out, he had a real talent for it. The high point of the car preparation in his garage probably came the night he used a circular saw to cut a square hole in the floor to accommodate the new transmission shifter. I had brought a new transmission with me from Michigan, one from a later-model Mercedes-Benz with the entire floor-shift linkage attached to it. We carefully measured exactly where in the floor of the car the shifter would be mounted, and Mark exuberantly let sparks fly as he repeatedly attacked the thick metal of the car's floorboard with the whirling saw. The man's capacity for destruction was

Mark's capacity for destruction is impressive as he cuts a hole in the car's floor for its new shifter. *Donna Moot*

impressive. Suddenly, I knew that it was all going to be okay. We would get the car finished in time, and somehow we would find the money. If Mark was capable of this, I figured together we would be capable of meeting all of the remaining obstacles that stood between us and the starting line in London. By the next time I returned to Ohio to work on the car, Mark had fabricated a clever bracket to hold the floor shifter in place.

Nothing was left to chance. The brake and fuel lines were routed inside the car to prevent them from being damaged by rocks. Mark had a special exhaust pipe extension fabricated in case we had to cross any deep rivers, and we welded extra gussets into the rear shock mounting brackets at the front and rear of the car. We built storage compartments under the front floorboards where we would store even more spare parts and a supply of energy bars to eat if we ever got desperate for food. Mark had made a deal with a company called NutriBiotics to supply us with the bars, and he kept insisting that they tasted great. I only hoped he was right. The ones he had for me to sample were pretty bad. We attached several light aluminum bars inside the car across the rear of the roof and strapped spare fuel and air filters to them. We bought a lightweight tent and strapped it just below the rear window, along with a pair of thin boards that could be used as splints in the event of a broken arm or leg. My wife, Loree, helped me outfit a comprehensive first aid kit that included drugs and ointments for almost every illness, insect sting or injury. Loree and I also went to Wal-mart and bought a jumbo-sized package of adult diapers. I felt a bit embarrassed about buying these and made loud comments in the check-out line about how they were for my grandfather. The reality was, if Mark or I got a bad case of the runs the rally wouldn't wait for us, and we would have to keep driving. The diapers, as distasteful as they seemed while standing in line at Wal-mart, had the potential to be pretty valuable if one of us got sick.

Mark insisted that we had to have a CD-player in the car. I was skeptical, especially after discovering that Mark's favorite band was the Pet Shop Boys. I reasoned that the racket inside the car while driving on unpaved roads and the constant jarring and dust would make a sound system impractical. Mark's solution was to install a marine-grade water-proof CD-player in the dash and a pair of speakers on the roll bar behind the front seats. It worked fine while sitting in Mark's garage, but I just wasn't sure how it would operate while driving across the Steppes of Asia.

With all of this work, both Mark and I began to feel real affection for our dumpy frumpy German sedan. After having led such a gentle life driving to Sunday dinner in the mountains of West Virginia, we wondered what it thought of its transformation into a razor-sharp around the world rally car.

In the midst of the preparations, Loree finished her residency at the University of Michigan and took a Hand Surgery fellowship at the University of Virginia in Charlottesville. This meant a move, and I was glad we had decided to do the final assembly of the car in Ohio. Our move didn't go at all smoothly thanks to an inept moving company, and I was glad that none of the items that they lost and damaged were parts needed for the rally car. It was a longer drive from Virginia to Mark's house in Ohio, and my visits became less frequent. We knew eventually I would need to bring the car to Virginia so that I could make final adjustments to the engine and suspension, and Mark redoubled his efforts to make the car road ready.

As the car neared completion, I began to have strange and disturbing premonitions that I might not return from the event alive. I am not usually visited by such thoughts, so I found them distressing. I didn't dare to share them with Loree or with Mark, but instead began selling off some of

Working out the details together made Mark and me a stronger team. *Donna Moot*

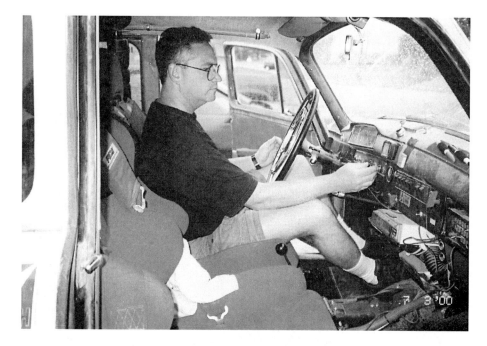

The interior of the car was modified for long distance travel. *Leroy Cole*

my collection of classic cars. My rationale was that it would be easier for me to dispose of my 1960 Morgan and my 1959 Jaguar XK150 Coupe than it would be for Loree to deal with after I had made her into a widow on this foolhardy endeavor. These were dark thoughts, but I couldn't shake them and I took special care to check the mounting of the seat belts, fire extinguishers and other safety equipment in our rally car when I was in Ohio working on it.

By November 1st the car was running and looked good in its new bright white paint. It then went to the American Sign graphics shop to be decorated with sponsors' logos. It came back looking like a circus wagon. It was not at all the dignified Mercedes-Benz automobile that would sweep into a chalet after a day of motoring along the Riviera. It looked like a refugee from NASCAR. Mark seemed so proud of the results that I tried not to let my disappointment show.

With endless phone calls to friends and acquaintances in the auto industry, I had managed to raise enough money to cover almost all of the new costs we had learned about at the Brooklands meeting. I also spoke with Maryalice Ritzmann in the Mercedes-Benz public relations department about putting our car on display at the New York International Auto Show in mid–April. This would give extra value to the sponsors whose

Top: Our classic car looks like a NASCAR stocker with all of its graphics. *Bottom:* Our car looked impressive prior to the start on the Mercedes-Benz stand at the New York Auto Show.

names were emblazoned on it. As the show was in late April, it would also mean our car would need to travel by air to London for the start. Mercedes-Benz was willing to undertake this cost in return for displaying the car on their stand, and letting them take care of this was another detail I could leave for someone else to worry about.

There was an almost endless stream of other details to attend to before the start. We eventually brought the car to Virginia for testing and tuning. Loree and I lived in the country on a mountainside surrounded by dirt roads and off-road trails that were perfect for trial runs. After testing the car on rough dirt roads, it was clear that the shock absorbers provided by Bilstein needed to be revalved to carry the car's heavy load. The carburetors had been rebuilt by a reputable shop but leaked badly and needed considerable attention. Mark had done a thorough job of wiring new switches for lights and cooling fans and other accessories, but there were a few glitches to work out. Christmas and New Year's passed in a blur and the year 2000 began with dozens of tasks still to be completed. I was still visited by dark thoughts of my own mortality but did a good job of hiding them from my friends and family. It was clear that Ed and Beverly Suhrbier were facing just as many problems on the West Coast as they put the finishing touches on their own Mercedes-Benz, and we corresponded frequently via e-mail to compare progress.

As an evaluation of the Classic Rally Association, I flew to England and ran in the Monte Carlo Challenge Rally, driving James Wiseman's classic 1959 Alfa Romeo Guilietta Spider from London to Cannes. The roads were ice and snow covered, the guardrails non-existent, the organizers sadistic in their navigation and timing tactics, the other competitors brave, tough and savvy. A gentle jaunt in old cars? In Europe you snug your belts, tighten your lug nuts and get ready for a wild ride. Thinking about the classic Monte Carlo Rally, among the toughest events on the European classic rally scene, can make drivers and navigators pale beneath their tanning-booth skin tones.

Just as in the old days, the Monte had several different starting locations around Europe. The majority of the 220 or so entrants start at Brooklands in England, but starting in places like Oslo, Stockholm, Ypers, Belgium, St. Moritz, Switzerland, and Noordvick, Holland, was also possible. Strangely, the rally didn't actually end at Monte Carlo in the principality of Monaco. Thanks to a dispute between Philip Young and the Automobile Club de Monte Carlo, the event actually ended in nearby Cannes. No matter, as the snow-covered roads to the French Riviera were the real test. At the start at Brooklands were Bentleys, MGs, Triumphs, Volvos, Mercedes-Benz's, Porsches and a host of other pre-war and post-war cars from rallying's golden age. Several of them were driven by people who would also compete in the Around the

James Wiseman (right) and I ran the 2000 Monte Carlo Winter Challenge in his 1959 Alfa Romeo to check out Philip Young's rally organization.

World rally. There was little time to socialize, however, as the organizers had devised a devious way to make the competition tight. At the first control in the morning, Wiseman and I were a half hour early. This was allowable as it gives teams time to purchase gasoline or work on their cars. The second control, we were ten minutes early. On the third control we arrived exactly on time after a spirited drive. This was how the organizers add pressure, making it more and more difficult to remain on time. Anyone with a problem of any sort would lose time and gain a penalty.

Then there were the regularity sections. From time to time, the organizers added a special section, timed to the second. Usually, it was a tough mountain pass or particularly twisty section of road. The object in a regularity is to stay exactly on time throughout the section, as competitors are not told where the section will end. The speeds seemed quite moderate, 50 kph or 31 mph for example. But maintaining 30 mph on an ice-covered mountain road with cliffs, tunnels, hairpin turns and few if any guardrails is not for the faint-hearted. Everyone, even the front-runners, lost time on the regularity sections, and the field was beginning to spread out.

On the second night of the event the route began in the mountains around Valence. In theory the first cars in this group would finish around 11 P.M., which meant if we stayed on time we could be to our hotel by half-past midnight. We did not stay on time. About 10 P.M. while sliding along a fast dirt road, I noticed the lights had suddenly dimmed. We turned off the heater and map-light, but soon the engine began to sputter as the electric fuel pump wasn't receiving enough juice from the dying electrical system. With its last few volts, the car stuttered to a stop at a control on the top of a ridge. It was dark and cold, and we were far from anywhere. Upon opening the trunk, we found the battery had split in two and spilled acid all over our gear. Competitors who checked into the control after us asked if they could help, but nobody carried a spare battery.

Meanwhile, a local farmer who had come to watch the event mentioned to the Dutch timing crew that he had a battery in an old car behind his barn. The Dutch timers began to pack up, their job finished for the night, but they let me wait inside their warm camping trailer as it had gotten very cold outside. When Wiseman and the farmer returned with new battery, it wasn't new and it wasn't charged. We connected up jumper cables and tried jump-start the car from the Dutch worker's vehicle, but something was wrong with our charging system and the car wouldn't keep running. Finally, our new Dutch friends produced a portable jump-start pack and we connected it to the battery. The car ran when connected to this device so we decided to drive on using the portable power source to run the engine and lights. We had about 50 miles to go. If we were to quit now, we would be out of the rally.

It was 2 A.M. and about 40 miles later when the engine stopped again. We were stuck by the side of the road in a tiny town in France, but we had one more chance. Using a cellphone, we reached the sweep vehicle. They were still out on the course helping stranded competitors. They were not far from us and would pick us up on their way to the hotel. I marveled at the sharp contrast between the friendly people manning the sweep vehicle and the sometimes-sour disposition of the organizers. The sweep guys were our heroes. They drove the same route as the rally cars, keeping to roughly the same schedule while driving a cumbersome former Camel Trophy Land Rover Discovery. They were willing and able to fix almost anything and were the guys who would pull you out should you drive over a cliff.

By noon the next day we had a new generator and voltage regulator to match our brand-new battery from the local Bosch distributor. One of the good things about the Monte Carlo Rally is that you can lose time by skipping controls yet still remain in the event as long as you reach certain critical main controls. After careful route plotting on a map we chose a point to rejoin the rally and continued on. The roads remained difficult, but the lack of fresh snow meant many of the cols (or passes) were mostly wet or dry pavement with just an occasional patch of ice. Still, there were exceptions and the organizers found opportunities for winter driving, especially during regularity sections. After the town of Gap, the rally covered many of the legendary cols from previous Monte Carlo Rallys. Sometimes four or five rally cars would drive together; at other times the roads seemed completely deserted, with headlights and driving lights piercing the murky darkness, driver and navigator oblivious to huge drop-offs just beyond their edge of perception.

On the outskirts of the town of Cannes our heater core burst, spraying the inside of the car with hot antifreeze coolant. After the system cooled, we bypassed the heater and borrowed water from an astonished pharmacist to refill the radiator. We reached the finish exhausted and reeking of coolant. Two-time Monte Carlo Rally winner and rally legend Erik Carlsson and his equally-legendary rally-driving wife, Pat Moss, were the guest speakers at the black-tie dinner. He is one of my heroes, and I had begun to understand just what it must have been like for him to win rallies on these same roads back in the 1960s. I was also impressed by the event. Even if Philip Young was often grumpy, his Classic Rally Association could deliver the goods. I learned a lot from my Monte Carlo adventure. The need for self-reliance was paramount, and I was sure that it was a lesson I would need to apply when driving around the world. The most important thing I learned was, aside from the mechanics in the sweep vehicle, I could expect little in the way of assistance or sympathy from Philip Young and his organizing team if things went wrong.

Back home, Mark checked the U.S. State Department reports on the countries we would be visiting in the former Soviet Union. I wished he hadn't. It didn't look good. Our government didn't particularly encourage travel in the region by Americans. Robbery, terrorism and poor medical care were all cited as concerns. Meanwhile, Chris Jensen looked over our rally car and had a few suggestions. One was that we place heavy metal screens over the windows and windshield to protect them from rocks thrown by hostile people at the sides of the road. With his experiences in Asia and Africa, it was a worthwhile suggestion, but we didn't have the time to do it. Instead, we included in our spares a large piece of rigid clear plastic cut to the shape of the windshield opening. If we lost the windshield we figured we could tape this piece into place to keep us in the rally. Chris also strongly recommended that we consider buying kidnapping insurance. This sent a chill up my spine. What had we gotten ourselves into? Mark made some phone calls and found that for $500 each we could get insurance that would cover up to a million dollars of ransom and provide a professional negotiator. Our budget was still pretty tight, but this seemed like a good idea. The one catch was that we weren't allowed to make it known that we had the insurance, lest we become more enticing targets to kidnappers. Special medical insurance was available from the organizers that would provide emergency evacuation by air in case of illness or injury. The countries we would visit would have little in the way of medical care and it would be imperative to get out as quickly as possible in the event of a medical emergency. I visited my local health department and set up a schedule of 16 injections for everything from rabies to Japanese encephalitis.

It was during this time that I began to have an understanding of just how large an undertaking the rally would be. I would be gone for three months. During this time my monthly columns in *Automobile Magazine* and *European Car* would continue. This meant working several months ahead to keep my name in print. I also made commitments to provide weekly updates on our own Web site, the Web site of *Automobile Magazine* and another one called iStyletv. I knew that this would be difficult, but I felt I needed to provide everyone back home with news about the adventure as it was happening. It would be a long trip around the world, but I was determined that my friends and family along with all of our team sponsors would be a part of it. There was historical precedent for this. Luigi Barzini had ridden with Prince Borghese on the winning Italia during the 1907 Peking to Paris race. During the 1908 New York to Paris race, the winning Thomas team from the U.S. carried several journalists at different stages of the race. Using the telegraph, from the most remote parts of the planet, reports of the team's adventures went out to newspapers around the world. If pioneering journalists could do it in 1908, I thought I should be able to do as well in 2000. I considered getting a satellite telephone but after speaking with AT&T in the U.S. I was assured that my tri-band mobile cellular telephone from Europe would do the job, even in China.

By now I was looking at the maps daily, memorizing the relationship between the Caspian Sea and Turkmenistan, or pinpointing exactly where Samarkand was located. On flat maps, it all looked straightforward. Around that time I happened to be watching a television program about space exploration showing a view of the earth from an Apollo lunar spacecraft. In a flash I understood that forty other teams of crazed enthusiasts and I would soon be driving old cars all the way around that shimmering blue and green orb. It seemed like madness.

It was finally time to bring the car to New York City for the press days of the New York Auto Show. My initial plan was to haul the car on a trailer from Charlottesville to the show in New York City, but this suddenly seemed wrong. The car would soon be driven completely around the world. What better way to start it off than by driving it to New York? The drive was notable for the heavy rain and huge trucks but was uneventful. In the Jacob

Javitz Center the car sat on the Mercedes-Benz stand next to current new S-Class sedans. It looked good: kind of mean and purposeful with its high ground clearance, tough skid plates, even with its circus wagon graphics. Maryalice Ritzmann from Mercedes-Benz and Sue Sizemore from Bridgestone Firestone were there to offer me moral support. Walking around on the show floor, I was hailed by several of my colleagues in the motoring press. They wished me luck, though most claimed that I was insane for even wanting to go on such an adventure. Were they jealous? Most figured that Mercedes-Benz had done all of the work, and now I was just waltzing in to drive the car. I tried to explain the reality to a few of them, but it was clear that the automotive press corps was not going to understand the time and effort that Mark and I had put into the project. It would probably never occur to most of them to undertake such a project on their own. Sometimes I couldn't understand myself why we had done it. After the show, the car was taken by trailer from Manhattan to the Newark airport. At the airport it was loaded onto a cargo aircraft and shipped to London. All was finally in place for the adventure to begin.

4

The Beginning in Europe

New York, February 12, 1908
"Our Thomas was the last to pull away from Times Square as a
matter of national politeness, but before Broadway became the
Albany Post Road, now, roughly, Highway 9, we overtook and passed
not only the Sizaire-Naudin but the Motobloc and the Protos as
well."
— George Schuster with Tom Mahoney, *The Longest*
Auto Race, New York to Paris 1908, 1966

"There was a tremendous sense of fun and excitement in the air
and a feeling that we were all on the threshold of one of motoring
history's great, and as yet untold, adventures. It was almost a relief
when 2:26 P.M. ticked by; Graham Hill, the 1968 World Champion
driver, dropped the flag and we rolled down the starting ramp on the
first few yards of our 11,000-mile journey. Either we had everything
with us or we didn't — it was too late to worry about it now."
— Innes Ireland, *Sideways to Sydney*, 1971

Perhaps the most famous of all Chinese proverbs is the one about a
long journey beginning with a single step. After two and a half years of
preparation and thousands of steps, I arrived in England four days before
the beginning of the rally around the world. My scary premonitions of
death and disaster were still with me, but there was nothing to be done
about them. Mark, his wife, Donna, and their two daughters had arrived a
few days earlier and had cleared the car out of customs at Heathrow airport. It was then transported to a Mercedes-Benz dealer called Normand
City near the starting line on Tower Bridge. The people at Normand were
great; they gave us a corner of their busy shop floor to complete our final
preparations on the car. The car looked purposeful with its bright graphics and our rally number 76 emblazoned in black on each side. We checked

54

everything over carefully, since our next chance to do any work on the car would be a week later in Greece. On Friday, we brought the car to the headquarters Thistle Tower hotel and joined the other cars gathering for the start.

Ed and Beverly Suhrbier, our friends from California who were driving car number 48, a 1959 Mercedes-Benz Cabriolet, invited us to a picnic in Hyde Park on Saturday afternoon. Ed and Bev had determined to do the send-off in a big way and had invited several dozen family members and friends to eat fried chicken by the lake. Among Team Suhrbier's guests was the classic Mercedes-Benz expert from California who had restored their car and prepared it for the event. The car was a pretty cream and China red; but privately, I was concerned about the lack of any important spare parts. They had elected to retain standard drum brakes and stock suspension and shock absorbers, and I feared that critical spare parts such as brake shoes might be hard to come by once the event had started. Their restoration expert was almost cocky about how well he had prepared their car, so I left the subject alone. It was a beautiful spring day blessed with sunshine and warmth, and the realities of the long drive ahead seemed far away.

On the day before the start, in the parking lot of the Royal Mint, we finally saw the other competitors' vehicles. They were lined up for inspection to ensure that they met the extremely detailed preparation rules. Any semblance of order quickly dissolved into chaos as highly competitive overachiever drivers pushed ahead to be among the first through the process. Was this to be a preview of the type of behavior we could expect for the entire event? Considering how detailed the written rules had been, the technical inspection itself was rather casual. Clearly, all of the cars that had made it to London were going to be allowed to start. Entrants who were obviously cheating or who had gone beyond what the rules allowed would somehow be dealt with later. After spending so much effort and money to make sure our car met the letter of the rules, Mark and I were disappointed that things weren't more rigorous. We probably could have stuffed a Chevrolet V-8 engine under the hood and gotten away with it. Other competitors expressed the same thoughts, and the organizer's disappointingly lax inspection would cause bad feelings later on in the rally.

The incredible variety of classic vehicles was impressive. There were mighty pre-War Bentleys and a diminutive Citroen 2CV from Chicago. There were sports cars from the fifties and sixties and a smattering of American cars from the thirties. Henning Ulrich, a dentist from Germany and his Polish mechanic, Klemens Suchocki, brought the only diesel powered car, a 1958 Mercedes-Benz 190 D sedan. Actually, there were a lot of Mercedes-Benz models, including several coupes similar to the one we had wanted to bring. Apparently Philip Young wasn't able to persuade all of his

Nine days into the rally, the Hilton parking lot in Istanbul looked like an automotive war zone.

entrants to go with older, slower and simpler cars. There was an air of excitement; everyone knew that the next day's start would be the beginning of an epic adventure.

Monday morning, May 1st, 98 cars gathered on London's Tower Bridge. After two and a half years of sweat and toil, we were on the starting line of the rally. Actually, Mark was on the starting line with our car; I was in the Thistle Tower in my room being interviewed by National Public Radio. After months of discussions, NPR had decided at the last moment that my story would be interesting and agreed to do an interview from London before the start. The host of Morning Edition, Bob Edwards, asked what it would be like to drive across some of our globe's most remote highways. I told him a little about how we had prepared ourselves and about some of the other competitors. After the interview, I promised the NPR people that I would call them again in nine days from Istanbul for an on-air update. Finally, 45 minutes before the start, I was able to join Mark on the bridge. We had been told to line up by numerical order and there were predictably some last minute rearrangements, but all went reasonably well.

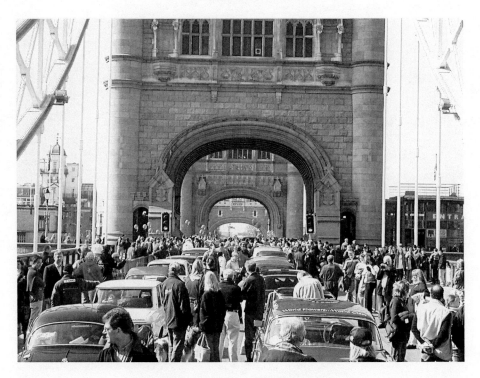

The starting line-up on Tower Bridge.

A huge and enthusiastic crowd had gathered. It wasn't quite the 250,000 people who had gathered in New York on February 12, 1908, for the start of the original around the world event, but a crowd of perhaps 10,000 was onhand. In addition to friends and family, thousands of vintage auto and adventure enthusiasts came to see us off. There had been some rumors that anarchists were going to stage an organized demonstration against the conspicuous wealth that the rally represented. The concept of organized anarchists seemed funny to us, but none were seen on London's Tower Bridge that morning.

At 10 A.M., racing legend Sir Stirling Moss flagged away the first car on the Around the World in 80 Days Motor Challenge. It was an extraordinary 1913 Locomobile Type 48. One that looked more like a locomotive than an automobile. How could anyone expect to drive something like that around the entire globe?

Next came a pair of Rolls-Royce Silver Ghosts. Large and stately, the epitome of that oh-so-British manufacturer's craft. Then came our American pals Chick and Bob in their 1929 Marmon sedan. It took two men who were quite certain of their manhood to drive something so shockingly pink.

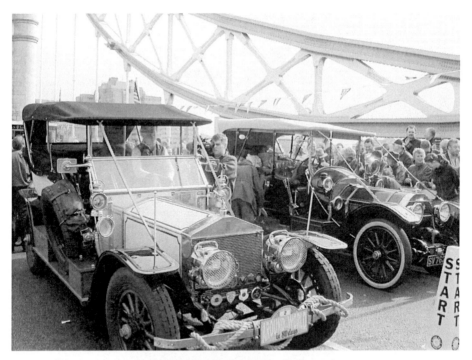

Top: The earliest cars started first: Here are cars number 1 and 2, a 1912 Locomobile (right) and a 1913 Rolls Royce Silver Ghost. *Bottom:* A crowd of perhaps 10,000 saw the racers on their way.

I slid my car's transmission into first gear, and we moved forward in line onto Tower Bridge, through the crowds, and to the starting line at the other end of the bridge. Moss, always known for his sartorial sensibility, was nattily dressed in coat and tie, and I made some inane comment to him, asking if he'd remember me to his famous brother-in-law — and one of my biggest motorsports heroes — the Swedish rally driver Erik Carlsson whom I had seem in January in Cannes. Sitting across from me in the passenger seat, Mark immediately accused me of name-dropping, but I couldn't think of anything else to say to Moss. I was nervous. I had spent so much time and a fortune of other people's money to be able to sit here on the starting line on Tower Bridge. Moss smiled vacantly at my comment and turned away to talk to a bystander. He had figured me for an idiot; I certainly didn't blame him.

The minute ticked away until Moss counted down the seconds from five and lifted the starting flag. I revved the engine and, slipping the clutch slightly, lurched over the line as Mark Rinkel and I in car number 76 began our adventure on the world's longest-ever motoring competition.

The route on the first day took us through the English countryside toward the ferry crossing at the White Cliffs of Dover. I kept reminding myself to drive on the left side of the road. I was following a 1968 Mini that was entered in the London to Istanbul Challenge, an event that Philip Young had created to run along with the Around the World and London to Beijing events. As I approached a roundabout, I looked right and saw the traffic was clear. Ahead of me however, the Mini had stopped at the circle entrance. I jammed my brakes to the floor and skidded to a stop inches from the Mini's rear corner. Less than 10 kilometers into the event, and already I had nearly caused an accident. Shakily, I put the car into gear and made a silent promise to myself to be ever vigilant, at least until we were out of England. Mark, to his credit, made no comment, but he must have been wondering what he was in for. In each town we visited hundreds of people stood on the sidewalks and leaned out of pubs cheering for us. It was an extraordinary feeling to be at the center of so much attention and high spirits. Getting the car to the starting line had been an ordeal, and now we were actually underway.

Arriving at Dover in time for the 1:30 P&O Ferry to Calais, we loaded our cars and went in search of some of the other teams. For some the first day had not been so easy. The locomotive-like 1913 Locomobile of Seeley and Michelmore, car number 1, was out of the event with a blown engine within 40 miles of the start. This was eerily similar to the 1908 event when the single-cylinder Sizaire-Naudine driven by Auguste Pons broke its axle and retired 40 miles after starting at West 43rd Street and Broadway in New York. We also heard that American Bill Borchert Larson, in car number 2,

The rally waits at Dover for the P&O Ferry to Calais.

a 1914 Rolls Royce Silver Ghost, had missed the start due to illness. He sent his co-driver, Terry Maxon, to drive to Istanbul with a substitute navigator who had seemingly volunteered impulsively from the assembled crowd to join him in the car. For some reason, whether by Philip Young's design or by happenstance, this story was taken up by the British press and became the primary story of the rally for a week. It probably helped that the volunteer was a reasonably attractive blonde English woman named Julie Holdcroft. To those of us on the rally, it was an insignificant wrinkle. The press jumped on it, making it the story of the rally to the outside world. We never did really find out if the story had been orchestrated by Young to generate more press. Terry Maxon, an American from California, wouldn't be drawn out on the subject. Borchert Larson meanwhile had made plans to join up with his yellow Rolls Royce again a week later in Istanbul.

From Calais, it was a mad scramble off the boat and on the road. Nobody expected to take any penalties on the first day, and the timing was overly generous to allow teams a chance to get to Chantilly, north of Paris. The route which went through central France was wide open, and it was easy to make good time. Those with fast cars made the most of it to try to get to Chantilly early to ensure a good night's sleep before the next day's driving. Nigel and Paula Broderick in their 1967 Mercedes-Benz 250SL sports car made it faster than anybody else. The organizers had made it clear before the start that they wanted competitors to follow the prescribed route. But then, inexplicably, the night before the start they announced that there would be no secret checks on the route. This meant cars could follow whichever course they wanted, as long as they visited the controls outlined in their route books. The Brodericks and several others bypassed the route through most of England and avoided the ferry crossing altogether by taking the Channel Tunnel. There was some grumbling from teams who had run the prescribed route. There was nothing technically illegal with what the Brodericks and the others had done, but some felt like it wasn't in keeping with the proper spirit of the event. None of this would have happened if the organizers had stuck to their original rules and all of us would have followed the same route.

In the 1908 event it hadn't taken long for trouble to start. On the route through upstate New York to Buffalo the teams hit heavy snow and icy con-

Almost from the start, the 1908 event was beset with heavy snow and tough going. *Courtesy of the Detroit Public Library, National Automotive History Collection*

ditions. It made the travel difficult, but nothing would compare to the six-foot snowdrifts that they encountered outside of Chicago. It took thirteen and a half days to drive the 1,400 miles from New York to Chicago; the teams spent eight days driving the last 256 miles. They tried everything to get through including dragging the cars with horse teams and flat-bottom sledges. Progress was finally made by digging with shovels and inching the cars forward through the drifts. In desperation, the Thomas team asked for and received permission to drive on the plowed roadbed of the New York Central Railway, and they were the first car into Chicago.

Ninety-two years later, the conditions we faced were far more hospitable. The Chateau de Montvillargenne in Chantilly, with formal gardens and a long imposing entryway, was most impressive from the outside. A cold buffet was set out for a pricey $18 per person, and as there was nothing else to be found for miles in any direction, we had no other choice. Our room in the chateau was directly over the kitchen, and the staff loudly complained in French about their dishwashing duties long into the night. Later in the evening the local tomcat decided it would be a fine night for romance and chose to sing beneath our window. I couldn't sleep, and my head was pounding. One day into the event and I was already searching my overnight bag for sleeping pills and headache medicine.

The second day was another easy one, just a warm-up for the difficulties that were sure to come. It was so easy, in fact, that at the end of day two, we were among fifty-three other cars that shared first place. Cars arrived that evening in the charming town of Aix-les-Bains, a regular stop on the Monte Carlo Rally. I had been here in January on Phillip's Monte Carlo Challenge Rally and remembered the general layout of the town. Even so, it took us several tries to find the hotel; and by the time we arrived the frustration in our car had risen to a high level. The route instructions out on the rally roads were good, but the last few kilometers into town and to the finish were awful. This was a pattern that would be repeated throughout the event. We had a minor speed test in the center of the city by the lake in the shadow of the Jura Mountains, but it did nothing to change the results. Mark and I had a good and uneventful day—the kind we hoped would recur.

Unlike the 1908 event which was a race, our competition was organized as a rally. Each morning, each car was given a start time for the day. On the precise minute we were assigned to leave, our Route Card was stamped and signed by a rally official. We then began driving over a prescribed course, following route instructions that would deliver us to our next control point. We were given an exact amount of time to cover this distance, and although we could arrive at the control early, we weren't allowed to check in until exactly on our assigned minute. If delayed,

Top: A field of flowers behind our intrepid Mercedes in central France. *Bottom:* A village scene in France; this could easily be 1939!

you were given a penalty in the amount of time that you were late to check in.

Sometimes the route was easy and traffic was light, so we arrived early and had time to refuel the car or have a snack. Sometimes the roads were narrow, and it was a challenge to drive fast enough to stay on time. Sometimes it was impossible. After five or six controls were reached during the day, we would make the final control for the day, usually located at the hotel where we would be staying. To the uninitiated, it might seem that if you were going to drive an old car all the way around the world, you would take the easiest roads possible, but that's not how the game is played. Most of the roads the organizers chose were rural two-lane routes that had little or no traffic. Sometimes they were dirt roads or even goat tracks, depending upon how devious the organizers felt while setting up each day's run.

The third day promised to begin the competitive sections of the rally. We would be traveling through southern France and then through the Frejus Tunnel and across the border into Italy. The roads we were facing were smaller and more difficult. All was going well for Mark and me, and we were looking forward to the three closely timed tight and difficult sections. The first section was paved, but barely a lane wide. I threw the big Mercedes into the corners with abandon and was rewarded with nearly perfect handling. The balance of the car was impressive, and I silently thanked the effort that I had put into getting the spring rates and shock absorbers absolutely right. We began passing other competitors. I was driving the car aggressively, diving into corners under braking and hounding cars ahead until they let me pass. I was being reckless and taking bigger chances than I normally might while driving on a rally. The reality was that, as well as it handled, I was upset with our choice of car. The Mercedes-Benz Coupe would have been perfect on these roads, but instead I was driving this white whale of a sedan. It was underpowered, especially with the low compression cylinder head we had installed, and I was determined to show despite it all that I could drive the beast and keep up with the newer more agile cars. Pride inevitably goes before a fall, and all my fancy driving was for naught. About halfway through that first section in the Ligurian Hills, our car began to misfire and eventually to run on only three of its six cylinders. Suddenly we could barely climb the hills, and all of the cars we had passed before roared past us. I could stay with cars in the downhill sections by driving like a wild man, but we were hopeless on any hill. There was nothing to do but to press on; stopping would cost us more time. We lost three minutes on that section, three on the next and a disheartening nine minutes on a long uphill grind. Following the third section, I opened the hood, removed the carburetor float chamber and found a sticking float valve. It was such a simple thing, yet it had cost us fifteen minutes in penalties. Still,

Following another Mercedes rally car in the French Alps.

it could have been worse. David Stonely and Dennis Pomfret in a 1964 Austin Healey 3000 had misjudged the road while overtaking one of the pre–War Rolls Royces. They spun off the wet pavement and went backwards over a cliff, falling more than a hundred feet as the car crashed into rocks and trees. They were shaken but neither was seriously injured; their car however was a mess and they were unable to continue. Others faced problems, too. American Bill Secrest, with his 28-year-old daughter, Kelly, was in a borrowed 1935 Chrysler Airflow. The car's wooden floorboards caught fire due to an over-heated exhaust and they dumped all of their drinking water onto the flames to put them out. Team Suhrbier and others experienced brake problem as they ran the Italian hills past Genoa south along the coastline to Portofino. Ed Suhrbier had broken a rear shock absorber, and I lent him one of my spares to keep him in the event. I am sure that Ed's confidence in his smug Californian mechanic was beginning to wane.

After fixing the float in our carburetor we jumped on the Autostrada, and rushing through heavy traffic, arrived at our seaside resort for the overnight halt. The town was beautiful, and the hotel overlooked the harbor. In fact, of all the places we stayed on this adventure, Santa Margherita ranked

Typical Alpine roads of France and Northern Italy.

as the most spectacular. Mark went straight up to our room while I gassed the car and put it in a safe parking spot. I spent some time checking the car over and arrived at the hotel room about 45 minutes later. Mark was sitting on a chair on the balcony of our room. Before him were three empty beer bottles. "I bought one for you and two for me," he said. "Then after I had finished both of mine and you still weren't here, I drank yours, too." Later, sitting on the hotel veranda we had a wonderful Italian meal with an excellent Pinot Grigio to make up for the day's problems.

The next day would be a long one as we left the West Coast of Italy and drove across to the Adriatic coast to Ancona to catch a ferry-boat to Greece. It was hot and sticky and the weather wasn't helped by the heavy traffic near Pisa. If this was the organizer's attempt at adding scenery to the event it was a failure; far in the hazy distance we could just make out the famous tower standing at its defiant angle. Day three included our first gravel section. We followed car number 75, the 1964 Lancia of Roberto Chiodi and Rita Degli Esposti from Italy. We started on pavement and followed a long downhill stretch with a right turn onto a badly rutted and washboard gravel-filled section. We caught the Lancia just as we entered the gravel, and I didn't lift as we hit the first washboard. The skid plate at the front of the car took most of the impact and the front wheels rebounded high into the air. The next three impacts to the underside were just as hard as we rocketed past Roberto, who was carefully picking his way through the potholes and ruts. Once past the Lancia I backed off but still maintained a good pace through the rough section. We finished several minutes early and had to wait until our correct check-in time. The concern of being late pushed me to drive sections like this far too hard. Meanwhile, Roberto and Rita arrived in their Lancia, exactly on-time having driven the section at just the right speed to save their car. I understood that their way of carefully arriving on time was the better tactic; but all the same, driving like a maniac was fun; and we had built a strong car. Later that afternoon after crossing the low Apennine Mountains, we arrived on the eastern Italian coast for an overnight passage on the SuperFast III, an ultra-modern car and passenger ferry capable of speeds of more than 25 knots. We arrived at the docks about two hours before the boat was due to leave. I decided to check the front brakes and was shocked to discover that we had already worn through the front disc brake pads. I had anticipated the set lasting at least halfway around the world and here we had used them up in the first three days of the event. I pulled out our spare parts bin and grabbed a new set of pads. It was then that I discovered something even more distressing. The spare set of pads I had so carefully ordered and packed were the wrong ones for our car. They were about an inch too long to fit into the calipers and the mounting holes were drilled in the wrong locations. I sent Mark off in a taxi to Ancona to look for more brake pads while I started working with a hacksaw to cut the pads down to the proper size. It was agonizingly hot in the parking lot where hundreds of people milled around looking at the cars. I was sawing through high friction material, which quickly blunted the saw blades and wore them so thin that they could easily break. Each pad took half an hour to saw through and there were four pads. I began cursing Mark for taking so long. My arms were wearing out nearly as fast as the saw blades. I finished the job about fifteen minutes before the boat was due to sail, just as Mark returned from his taxi ride, unfortunately without brake pads. We pushed the car onto the ship and I found Peter Banham, one of the organizer's mechanics, and borrowed a drill to make holes in the proper locations in my makeshift brake pads. Temporarily we again had brakes.

We weren't the only ones with braking problems in Tuscany. Bill Secrest had a near total failure of the master cylinder in the big pre–War Chrysler, and mechanic Banham was busy changing the seals of the cylinder during the voyage. The problem had cost Secrest hours of penalty. Ed and Beverly had also picked up a significant penalty. One of the rear brake shoes in their 1957 Mercedes-Benz had come apart, leaving them with a brake pedal that went to the floor. With no spare brake shoes, they skipped most of the day's controls to drive to a Mercedes-Benz dealership looking for help. The best the dealer could offer was new brakes shoes from Stuttgart in about a week, so they struggled on to the ferry with only the slightest ability to slow their car. Ed later confided that he felt he had made a rookie mistake by trying to have the car fixed on that day when there were so many controls. Each missed control had cost them an hour and in the end the dealership hadn't been able to solve the problem anyway. The blistering fax that Ed sent to his mechanic in California made me happy I wasn't in the auto restoration business.

As the ferryboat passed close to the Albanian coast and approached the Greek shoreline, I was able to call home on my cellular phone. My wife, who had been monitoring our progress on the organizer's web site, wanted to know all about the blonde woman who had ridden across Europe in the early Rolls Royce. At first I was at a loss to understand what she was talking about. The blonde who had joined Terry Maxon on the rally on a lark was inconsequential to those of us in the rally. The big old Rolls was poorly prepared and had spent most days on the back of a flatbed truck being transported to the evening's destination. Philip Young had spun the story to the press and on his web site as the most important part of the trip. Julie Holdcroft, a 37-year-old hairdresser had become a minor celebrity in the U.K., and Mr. Young was going to keep feeding the story as long as he could. It wouldn't be the last time that the description of events given to the outside world didn't match the reality that we were living.

The ferry docked at 1:30 in the afternoon in Igoumenitsa in Southern Greece, and after disembarking, the route took us north through the mountains. Many of the roads were the same as those used by the famous Acropolis Rally, roads known for their ability to destroy the best factory-prepared rally cars. The scenery was spectacular; the roads were cut into the side of the cliff faces. Down in the valley we could see work progressing on a new modern highway that would eventually replace the mountain route we were driving. The new road would make driving quicker and safer, but the views would be nowhere near as wonderful.

Not long after leaving the ferry, we made a mid-afternoon lunch and fuel stop. The parking lot of the gas station was soon filled with rally cars, and the lunch counter did a brisk business. Everyone was waiting for their exact minute to restart the rally.

After lunch, the route continued along the main road for a short distance until it reached a control point just before the first gravel section near the Katara Pass. As I pulled away from the control, I noticed a dark blue Jaguar XK140 Coupe sliding into the control behind us. They should have

A brief fuel stop in Greece.

been several spots in front of us, so I figured they had gotten lost and were now running late. The route followed the highway for a couple of kilometers and then turned right onto a minor side road. Just as we reached the turn-off, the blue Jaguar caught up with us. Mark said the road would turn to dirt in about ten kilometers, so I moved over and allowed the Jaguar to pass, figuring his low-slung sports car would be much faster on the pavement section than our big sedan. As we rounded the next turn, the road changed to gravel and dirt. Damn. We were almost exactly on time at this point, and the average speed through the dirt section was posted at a rapid 45 mph. I quickly caught up with the Jaguar and honked my horn to let him know that I was there and expected him to let me pass.

The road now started uphill and widened slightly. I pulled out onto the loose gravel and began to pass. Just as I came alongside, the driver of the Jaguar swerved over to my lane, and I was forced to brake hard. My two left wheels skimmed the ditch on the side of the road. Now I was angry. I might have been driving like a madman, but the Jaguar was being driven by an idiot. I had given way when it was clear that his car would be faster on the paved section, so why was this guy holding me up on the gravel section where my car was clearly superior? I stayed a couple feet off of his bumper, blowing my horn and flashing my lights. Mark's rally computer told us we were losing time, but until the Jaguar let me pass there wasn't much we could do about it. Gravel and rocks the size of golf balls were flying from the Jaguar's rear tires. I feared our lights and windshield would be smashed by the fusillade. The dust kicked up was making it difficult to see the edges of the roadway. And although we soon passed Roberto and Rita's Lancia that had started a minute ahead of our car, I still couldn't find a way past the Jaguar. Then, as we neared to top of a ridge, we caught car number 74, a 1965 Mercedes-Benz Coupe driven by Ricardo Fox and Silvia Calderwood from Argentina. The road was slightly wider here, and I figured that as the Jaguar passed the Mercedes, I might just be able to pass the both of them. The dust was heavy and visibility was poor, especially with the two cars ahead churning up the road. Just as I went past the Mercedes, I noticed a road to the left.

"Should we have turned there?" I yelled at Mark.

"No," he answered. "Keep straight ahead!"

As I was bearing down on the Jaguar five seconds later Mark screamed, "We should have turned there! Go back! Go Back!"

Damn.

I braked hard to slow down to find a place to turn around. The road was little more than two lanes wide, and there were no turnouts. I looked in my rear view mirror and through the heavy dust saw the Mercedes behind us slowing down too. Or, at least that's what I thought I saw. I came to a stop and then turned the car broadside to the road to make a three-point turn around. Just then, out of the swirling dust came the big Mercedes-Benz Coupe. Its brakes were locked, and he was sliding straight at our front fender. For an instant I was sure he would miss us, then I heard a sickening crash as his right front bore into our left front wheel.

His bumper was pushed back into his tire. He had broken a headlight and had crunched his fender. As we were examining the damages, the Jaguar came roaring back up the hill. Apparently he realized that he had gone the wrong way, too. The driver never paused to check if we were all right but slid around the corner and continued on his rally. The bastard. The driver and navigator of the Mercedes Coupe were at a loss for what to do, so I slung our towrope around the front bumper of his Coupe and attached it to our tow hook. One good tug and the bumper was clear from the wheel. We tied their bumper on with a bungy cord and sent them on their way.

I figured that in the split second before the Mercedes Coupe hit us, its driver had three choices. He could have gone past the front of us, in which case he would have gone over a cliff. He could have gone behind us, and probably missed us altogether. Or he could have hit us, which is what he did. Still, it was a better option than going over the cliff. Besides,

Our poor Mercedes-Benz was badly damaged in our crash in the mountains of Greece.

I had caused his accident. When they were gone, we finally looked at our car.

The left front wheel was completely collapsed to a 45-degree angle and the fender was crushed against it. Mark figured we needed to get a tow truck and some help, but I knew the best plan would be to get the car out of these lonely mountains and back to the main road. We pulled away the fender with our hands and a hammer and decided to try to drive the car out. At first it seemed hopeless. The car pulled badly to the right and could barely turn left. Still, nothing seemed to be rubbing too badly. When we finally reached pavement, we decided to press on, but driving the car required enormous concentration just to keep on the road. Time after time a left hand bend would appear and we would have to nearly stop to negotiate it. Amazingly though, that tough old Mercedes-Benz held together, and we even arrived at the next time controls on-time. Ann and Peter Hunt, a couple from Scotland in a 1962 Austin Healey 3000, were behind us for a time on a twisty section. Later, Ann commented wide-eyed that if we drove that fast with a wrecked car, just how quickly did we drive the rest of the time? Mark later reminded me that at one point I had tensely said to him to never to tell anyone how fast we drove our damaged car. The price for driving with the demolished front suspension was the rapid wear of our light truck tires. They had proven to have stellar performance on the twisty roads of France and Italy, but could they stand up to the abuse our mangled suspension was giving them? By all rights, with the damage we had sustained, we should have been out of the rally. If we could make it to the end of the day we would have the next day off to make repairs.

Just after sundown we had one last gravel section to cover followed by a long run to the town of Thessaloniki. What we didn't know was the gravel section would be one of the toughest and most dangerous of the entire rally. Night had fallen, and the darkness added to our stress. The road started out with a quick run on pavement and then a switch to fast hard-packed dirt which wasn't too bad. Then the route took us onto one of the most appalling goat trails I have ever seen. I hit the entrance of the track fast — too fast for a car that could only steer in one direction. The right front wheel went into a huge hole, and the car rebounded left toward the edge of the roadway and a drop-off. At the last instant the car lurched to the right and back under my control. I managed to find first gear, and we began creeping up the narrow trail. As we came to a tight corner, I touched the brakes and the pedal went to the floor. A brake hose that had been damaged in our crash several hours earlier had finally failed. Under my breath I again cursed the driver of the blue Jaguar.

"No brakes!" I yelled to Mark.

He yelled for me to pull over.

"No," I countered, "we can keep going!"

Mark's voice sounded fearful. "You can't drive without brakes," he screamed.

I wasn't going to stop here. Not on the edge of a cliff and blocking the road.

"I'll use the handbrake," I said as coolly as I could manage.

Was this the fate that all of those creepy premonitions of death had been leading me to? We continued onward and upward. It wasn't too bad; the driving lights illuminated the cliff side and the road ahead. There was an ominous black void to our right.

Mark asked in a tight voice, "How are you doing?"

"Not very well," I had to admit.

I was beginning to worry. What was compelling me to keep going on this insane drive? We were traveling so slowly we would almost certainly receive a maximum penalty on the section anyway. I wanted to stop, but I couldn't. Not while there was a chance to keep the car moving forward.

"If you start to lose it, drive into the cliff," Mark advised, staring out into a thousand feet of blackness on his side of the car.

Right.

We arrived at a hairpin left turn. I turned the wheel as far left as I could and drove the right front fender into the cliff. I reached down and pulled on the handbrake. The car began rolling backward. The handbrake wasn't holding. This was bad. I quickly put the car back into first gear and used the clutch to hold it stationary. Carefully, I let the car slip backward against the clutch and cranked the wheel to the right as I tried to coax our big Mercedes around the tight hairpin without falling over the cliff that waited in the blackness inches behind our rear bumper.

It took four or five tries, but I finally managed to jockey the big car around the tight hairpin. All this time we had been climbing the side of a mountain ridge; and now we were nearing the top; but without a handbrake, our chances of controlling our speed on the descent seemed impossible. The road widened out at the top of the ridge, and I found a grassy spot wide enough to park the car to change the split brake hose. It was incredibly dark, but the stars shone brightly overhead, and I even saw a meteor as I replaced the fractured line. Every once in a while a late running rally car would grind past, and we would signal we were okay.

Finally, we had the car back together and continued on. We soon caught a slow moving Porsche that had driven past our repair site some moments earlier. They were halfway up the narrow lane, convinced they had gone the wrong way. Their car was perfect, and they were creeping along the road more slowly than we were. They flagged us down, and then wanted me to back up and turn around. Didn't they realize I couldn't turn left? I stood my ground and they finally backed past us with less than an inch to spare between our cars. Five kilometers later we emerged at the time control and headed straight to the night's finish in Thessaloniki. If we could arrive by our 1:07 a.m. scheduled arrival time, we would avoid the massive penalty for missing the day's finish control. I drove as fast as I dared, running over seventy miles per hour on a short stretch of four-lane highway and pushing through deserted villages. By now I was exhausted, but I had a sense of how to drive the mangled Mercedes and I didn't want Mark to take over. It wasn't that I didn't trust him, but I felt I had to do it myself. At one point I asked myself what I was doing, driving such a severely damaged car at such speeds. If something failed, the accident would be big. And yet I felt almost no fear, as if surviving that harrowing run over the dark mountains of Greece had exorcised whatever demons had possessed me. I was afraid that if I let Mark drive, whatever evil spells had been broken might suddenly reappear.

We arrived at the Macedonia Palace Hotel with two or three minutes

We drove this battered car for more than 100 miles at speeds over 70 mph.

to spare, and I parked the car behind the hotel in a lot with the rest of the rally cars. We had driven more than 200 kilometers with a car that looked like a candidate for a wrecking yard. Mark went to clock into the control and I just sat quietly for a few minutes, looking out over the dark Aegean Sea and trying to collect my thoughts, thankful that we had made it in. Hell, I was thankful to be alive. Our total penalty for the day was one hour and twenty minutes. Our biggest break was that the next day was our day off, and we could work on the car without penalty.

Before leaving the States, I had been given a list of Mercedes-Benz dealers around the world. While there were strict rules against pre-arranging service, Mercedes-Benz dealers had been notified that the rally would be passing through. The notification was primarily for the benefit of Claude Picasso, who was running a 1964 Mercedes-Benz 230 SL sports car that had been prepared by the workshops of the factory museum in Germany. We too had asked the people at Mercedes-Benz North America to send out some faxes on our behalf, and now we would be calling on the loose network for assistance.

In the morning I woke early and went downstairs to an empty hotel lobby. Mark was still in bed, and it was far too early for other rally teams to be awake. I felt cheerful and content, confirming that all of those previous premonitions of imagined death and disaster had been left behind during the reality of the disaster of the night before. My buoyant mood was dimmed somewhat by the sight of our poor wrecked Mercedes sitting in the parking lot. Somehow, I knew that everything was going to be just fine. No matter what it would take, I was going to complete this trip around the world, and nothing was going to stand in my way. I thumbed through our notebook of emergency contact numbers and found one for a Mercedes dealer in Thessaloniki, Greece.

Panayotis Koustelidis is the Service Manager at Ioannidis SA, the distributors of Mercedes-Benz in Greece. He is the father of four children and had lived in England and the Arab Emirates in his career working for Mercedes-Benz. He is also extraordinarily resourceful. He arrived at our hotel on the waterfront less than an hour after I called him. He looked at our car and decided immediately that he would open the workshop just outside of town. I followed him there, and as I drove I couldn't believe we had driven this thing so far and so fast the previous night. It was barely controllable. What had I been thinking?

Koustelidis called in two mechanics, and we took apart the old beast. The upper control arm on the left side was hopeless, a pretzeled mass of metal. It was clear we would need a new part. Koustelidis thought for a moment then took me in a Mercedes-Benz service truck to a special section of Thessaloniki where every imaginable car part can be found. As he explained, traders from Greece drive trucks to Germany and buy whole loads of used auto parts. Engines, suspensions, wheels, brakes and body parts are loaded into the trucks and then cross the borders as scrap metal. Once in Greece, the parts are sorted and sold from shops that are little more than holes in the walls. Most specialize in one type of automobile, with BMW, Mercedes-Benz and Volkswagen being the most popular brands. After several hours of searching a warren of parts caves, we found someone who knew someone who could get us the part we needed. He jumped on his motorbike to go across town to get the part; Koustelidis and I watched his store and drank Turkish coffee.

It was an interesting hour. Sitting on the shop floor was a 4.5-liter V-8 engine from an early-eighties Mercedes-Benz model. From the dust it had collected, it looked like it had been there for a long time. There just couldn't be much of a market for the powerful V-8 engine in this part of the world. What if we couldn't find the part to fit our forty-year-old Mercedes? Would we end up stranded in Thessaloniki for as long as that big V-8 had?

With little else to do, Koustelidis tried to explain his fellow countrymen to me.

"If I would tell you 'Death to America' today, I wouldn't mean any-

Almost any car part can be found in Greece, if you know where to look.

thing by it, and we could easily have a drink together tonight," he said. He admitted that even the Greeks don't always know why they do the things they do. "We are very emotional people, and just say what we feel at the moment; you can't take what we say seriously," he added.

What I was feeling at the moment was the need for an upper control arm for a forty-year old Mercedes-Benz.

After an amusing hour had passed, the man on the motorbike returned with the exact part that we needed. Back in the workshop, the mechanics had pounded the fender out so it no longer hit the tire. One mechanic showed me the brake hose I had replaced the night before. From the continuous rubbing on the tire, it had worn paper-thin; had we driven any distance further it would have worn through the rest of the way and we would have lost our brakes for the second time. They replaced that hose and Koustelidis even found a new set of front brake pads to replace the set I had cobbled together on the ferry dock in Italy. He refused any payment for all of his assistance, insisting that what we were doing by driving our gallant machine around the world was important for the honor of the company for which he had worked for so many years. How do you express gratitude to a man like that?

Our repaired car is ready to continue.

Back at the hotel, I pulled out a roll of white duct tape and covered the ugly gash on the side of our car. Mark's contribution was three Band-Aids from our first aid kit. As I had left so early in the morning to make the repairs, few of the other competitors had seen our car. Now they came by to comment on the hastily pounded out fender without knowing the full extent of the damage our car had suffered or the drama that had played out the night before. I noticed the Mercedes coupe that had crashed into us still had our bungy cord holding its front bumper in place; nothing else had been done to it during the day off. Mark had found a place to do our laundry and had spent the day talking with the other American teams. Many had spent the day off rebuilding their cars. Day five and already some cars in the parking lot looked rather banged up, ours included.

The next morning the route took us east once more into the low mountain range that lies between Greece and Turkey. After so many hectic days, and with my inner voice of doom silenced, I began to appreciate the scenes around us. It was beautiful.

Alexander the Great came this way in 300 BC to conquer Persia, and we were following the tracks his army had made. Originally I had vowed that I wouldn't get too caught up in the rally; I promised myself I would take the time to look around and appreciate the places we passed. If you didn't count the Mercedes workshop in Thessaloniki, I hadn't done much of that thus far. We followed the route through small villages and towns, the buildings bleached white in the hot sun. Lunch coincided with a checkpoint on the waterfront in the town of Porto Lagos. Old tramp steamers sat rusting at the docks as rally cars filled the parking lot and overflowed onto the street. The town was filled with children who came to see the classic cars and their foreign crews. Little cafés served salads with feta cheese. The scene looked like a postcard from the Greek Tourism Board. Suddenly there seemed to be lots of time. The sun shone brightly and everyone ate ice cream and enjoyed the warmth. For many, this is what they had come for, and the rally they had imagined had finally started. In the afternoon, a smooth gravel section near the town of Kirki called for discretion. I drove slowly and carefully, mindful of doing more damage to our car. We hadn't even made it out of Europe yet; I wanted to see Asia and China! Our time through the overhanging olive trees was embarrassingly slow, and I brooded for the rest of the day over the

This sun-splashed seaside stop in Greece is what many people came on the rally to experience.

The small Greek villages were friendly to rally competitors.

decision to back off. Mark and I had agreed that the only chance we had was to drive slowly and conservatively and let the rest of the rally come back to us. But was it worth the embarrassment of being one of the slowest cars on the section? The leading car was Fred and Jan Giles from England in a 1968 Hillman Hunter, and they seemed ready to charge every road to the maximum. We were mired around 30th place. The Brodericks in their Mercedes SL sports car were right behind the Gilses, and the tension at the front of the field was pretty intense. Roberto and Rita in the Lancia had moved up to fourth with their careful driving tactics, but Rita was dismayed by how serious everyone was taking it. Privately, she told me she wished they were further back in the field so that they could enjoy the trip. I instantly offered to change places with Roberto and her. Anyone who thought that this would just be a gentle jaunt for old cars was mistaken, and even the avowed tourists were trying hard, pushing their cars to their limits to avoid penalties. In the supposedly more laid-back pre–War category, the competition between the leading 1937 Packard from Canada and the tiny 1952 Citroen 2CV from Chicago was equally fierce. Jim Walters in the Packard was setting times that would have put him among the leaders in the post-war category. Teams began to grumble about how legal some of the cars might really be as they struggled to match the times of the fastest cars. We had been on the road for almost a week. I had to wonder if this cutthroat attitude would continue for the next two and a half months.

It hadn't taken long for the competition to become intense in 1908, either. On the fourth day of that event, the teams were supposed to stop in Buffalo for an evening dinner. The Zust crew, having arrived in the morning, motored on after a quick breakfast and left a note for the others that read, "We will wait for you in San Francisco." The dinner was cancelled. Some teams were claiming that the Americans had cheated by having their car rebuilt at the Thomas factory as the race passed through Buffalo. This was not far from the truth; Schuster's Thomas had been extensively modified in the overnight stop at the factory in Buffalo. Additional ground clearance was obtained by switching front axles, and a new 35-gallon gas tank and a separate oil tank were added. Special suspension pieces were substituted for the production parts; and the car's heavy steel fenders were removed, replaced by aprons of heavy leather to protect the crew from the mud and spray from the wheels. In reality it was nothing that shouldn't have been done before the car had started the event, but it caused discontent among the other teams. Later, near Erie, Pennsylvania, the French crew of the De Dion car also complained at dinner that they had done all of the hard work by breaking the path through the heavy snowdrifts for the American Thomas team. Overhearing this comment, racing driver Montague Roberts—then competing with George Schuster on the Thomas—replied, "From now on you will know this is a race!" as he stormed out of the room. The Thomas was the first car to leave the next morning.

The border crossing between Greece and Turkey was our first encounter with the developing world. Leaving Greece was simple. Show your passport and car registration, and go on your way. A short drive through no-man's land brought us to the Turkish border. Kids, looking no older than 17, were toting machine guns and wearing their olive drab army uniforms. Our cars were herded into a fenced compound, and we began our entry into Turkey. First we stood in one line to get a stamp. Then we walked across the dusty parking lot to a squat building where four more lines covered immigration, customs, visas and everything else officials could think of. Occasionally, the required stamp cost several dollars, even though all of our visas had been arranged ahead of time. The building was soon jammed with several hundred sweaty rally competitors, and for many the process took hours. We were lucky to have arrived at the front of the pack, and Mark and I discovered that if we stood in different lines and passed the needed documents back and forth we could move more quickly. People grew wise to our trick, and soon everyone was doing the document shuffle.

From the border it looked like a quick trip along the coast of the Sea of Marmaris to the city of Istanbul. At least that's what the maps said. A four-lane highway punctuated with several tollbooths was the clear fast track to town. The tollbooths were a problem though, as they bottled up traffic. Soon we were creeping along, trapped as trucks, busses and cars all vied for their turn to pass though the gates. A special lane had been opened for the rally cars to pass through without charge, but nobody told the competitors about it. The frustration level grew high again, and every time we neared a tollbooth, Mark told me which lane I should be in. By Mark's view I seemed to consistently pick the wrong one.

Istanbul is notorious for its traffic problems, and finding our hotel in the middle of the night took more than an hour of circling and a huge amount of luck. I unfairly blamed Mark for being a poor navigator; but truthfully it was the cursed route book; it was worthless. More than one team, including Team Suhrbier, was wise enough to hire a taxi and follow it through the city to get to the Hilton rally headquarters.

We had driven all the way across Europe in nine days and were lucky to still be in the rally. I had driven well in some sections and like an idiot in others. I would need to do much better if Mark and I were going to make it to the finish. Whatever had caused my moodiness before the event had been lifted by my experience in Greece, and now I felt like the adventure was really just beginning.

Europe had been familiar; I had driven there many times before. Compared to what we were facing, the journey from London to Istanbul was like driving down to the corner for milk. Asia was another thing: it would be both new and filled with excitement and contained the prospect of even more drama. In Istanbul, Asia beckoned to us just across the Bosporus Bridge.

5

Another Day, Another Disaster

> *Oh, East is East, and West is West, and never the twain shall meet....*
> — Rudyard Kipling

> *The ferry boat crossing of the Bosporus was but a few miles away, and we all sensed that this water crossing marked the end of the continent we knew, and the start of the eastern world, which was a stranger. It was almost as if the adventure were just beginning.*
> — Innes Ireland, *Sideways to Sydney*, 1971

Before crossing the Bosporus and heading into Asia, there were a few things we needed to get done. Istanbul promised to be the last major city where we could count on Western goods and services until we reached Anchorage, Alaska, in more than a month's time. Our wild drive to Thessaloniki with our deranged front suspension had worn out two of our precious Bridgestone tires, and we now had no spares left. Mark was put in charge of finding two tires that would fit our 14-inch rims and getting the front end of the car aligned to ensure that we wouldn't continue to wear out the tires so quickly. He was aided in his task by representatives of the Classic Car Club of Turkey who had arranged for shops to be open and services to be available to the rally crews.

My journalism duties asserted themselves here at the edge of Western civilization, and I spent much of the day updating our web site and posting e-mail stories to the media outlets to which I had promised reports. This was a task that would need to be repeated every time we had a day off. And I finally had time to make a few phone calls home.

While talking to my 16-year-old daughter Jessica, she asked me, "Have you and Mark run out of things to talk about yet?"

"What do you mean?" I asked her.

"He is a dentist! How interesting can he be to talk to?"

My daughter had met Mark before we had left. Had she seen something in his personality that I hadn't?

I also spent a long time in Istanbul trying to reach National Public Radio in Washington for my promised second radio interview. Seemingly oblivious that I was calling from Turkey, I was placed on hold for long periods of time before finally receiving word that there would be no interview. The NPR producer suggested I try to call back again from China, and maybe something would work out. *Would it be so easy to call from China?* I told them I would try.

I took a break and walked through the car park which had been turned into a M.A.S.H. unit for classic automobiles. They were scattered everywhere, some receiving only minor attention while others needed major repairs. Head gaskets were being replaced along with wheel bearings and brake parts. The Brodericks had an electrical fire in their snazzy Mercedes-Benz sports car the night before in the traffic jam. They had come in on the end of a rope and were now trying to sort out the problem. Others were

Nine days into the rally, the Hilton parking lot in Istanbul looked like an automotive war zone.

trying to find parts to prepare themselves for what was to come. Team Suhrbier had brashly parked their stylish Mercedes-Benz Cabriolet in front of the hotel the night before, only to have it hit by a tour bus entering the parking lot. An ugly scratch ran the length of the front fender of Ed and Beverly's nearly pristine chariot. Still, it seemed minor compared to the mess of our and other's cars, and I was having a hard time working up much sympathy for their plight. Ed took command and demanded that the hotel send the Mercedes-Benz to a body repair shop. When it came back late that evening, you couldn't tell it had ever been hit.

Mark got back late in the afternoon with horror stories about Istanbul traffic. He had followed a local car club member to a garage where the car was aligned, and two new tires were found. Unfortunately they were Michelin light truck tires that were much larger in diameter than the ones we already had on the car. This meant that should we have a flat tire, we would need to change both tires on an axle to keep everything in balance. The new tires were so large that they didn't really fit into the special spare tire well we had built into the trunk area, and everything had to be repacked in order to get the trunk lid closed. I wasn't happy with the whole situation, but Mark insisted that these were the only 14-inch tires he could find in all of Istanbul. It didn't seem likely that we could drive all the way across Asia without having a single flat tire, and I wasn't looking forward to changing two tires when the inevitable happened. Still, our old Mercedes that had carried us this far was now fit again, and we felt ready to tackle the unknown.

Not everyone who started at London's Tower Bridge had set out to drive around the world. Philip Young had arranged three events to take place simultaneously, with nineteen entrants of the 98 starters going as far as Istanbul, having driven across the breadth of Europe. Thirty-nine more, including Ed and Bev of Team Suhrbier, would call it quits in Beijing after driving across Europe and Asia. For the nineteen teams ending in Istanbul, our arrival there marked the end of their event and a prize giving was held in their honor at the Istanbul Hilton. For these teams, the party, that included belly dancers and local musicians, was probably a big deal. To those of us driving around the world, the first week had been little more than a prelude. The London to Istanbul winner was a yellow 1966 Aston Martin DB6 driven by Adrian Pope and Julian Reddyhough of England, while the British father and son team of Stephen Harman and Steven Harman, Jr., in a 1952 MG TD won the pre–War category. With an early departure planned for the next day, it was hard for those of us who were continuing to build much enthusiasm for their party.

We departed from Istanbul and crossed into Asia over the sleekly modern Bosporus Bridge. The sun was shining, the sky bright and clear, the

Crossing the Bosporus Bridge into Asia.

bridge towering high above the sparkling blue waters of the straits. A small sign on the bridge indicated that we had left Europe behind us and had entered the continent of Asia.

In 1260, brothers Nicolo and Maffeo Polo set sail from Constantinople for the Crimean port of Sudak in search of new markets for their wares. Constantinople eventually became known as Istanbul and Nicolo Polo for his famous son Marco. Constantinople was ideally located for a trading center and for centuries was considered the western terminus of the Silk Road that brought goods from China. Today, it remains one of the busiest crossroads of commerce in the world.

We began a long run along a Turkish toll road. This four lane divided highway was just like those found in the U.S., and Turkish drivers weren't afraid to drive fast. We settled to a more sedate speed than that exhibited by the locals, who would honk and wave wildly as they sped past. After a couple hundred kilometers, the rally route diverted onto a secondary highway. At a rally time control, I casually opened the hood to do a quick check and was horrified to find the radiator catch tank full of coolant. This wasn't right. Worse, there were ominous bubbles coming from the radiator cap. A couple days earlier in Greece, we had noticed the temperature climbing suddenly and had diagnosed the problem as a sticking thermostat. We bypassed the defective unit, and the car had run cool ever since. This was serious, and the symptoms pointed to a blown head gasket. I borrowed a wrench and re-torqued the cylinder head, but I had a sinking feeling that things were not going well. Were we cursed? If only we had discovered this the day before, we could have repaired it in Istanbul, instead of in the wilds of Turkey. We refilled the radiator and set off carefully to our evening's stop at a beautiful resort on Boluabent Lake in Bolu, Turkey. We arrived at around 4 P.M. The car had run warmer than usual all through the afternoon. I knew what I had to do and a half-hour later began the process of changing head gaskets.

I am not a professional mechanic but have worked on cars all of my life, so I wasn't particularly concerned about the job at hand. Besides, Henning Ulrich had promised the aid of his professional mechanic co-driver Klemens to help things along. I laid out the tools and began taking things apart while Mark retired to drink beer at the open-air bar in front of the hotel. That pissed me off more than a bit. After an hour and a half, I was ready to pull the cylinder head off and called Mark for his help. Reluctantly he left his drinking buddies and grabbed the front of the head while I grabbed the rear as we pulled it from the engine. The news wasn't good. The gasket was blown in at least two different spots. Without any machine shop facilities I couldn't check if the overheating had warped the aluminum head. Mark went back to his beer as I grabbed our spare head gasket and began to put it all back together again. There wasn't really much else I could do.

Everything went pretty well, and by 9 p.m. I had the engine back together. I asked Klemens to double-check what I had done. Together we rechecked the engine for proper timing, and I was ready to try it. It started right away, but almost immediately made a horrible clattering noise. I shut it off and opened the valve cover to see if I could find the problem. To my horror, I discovered two of the camshaft supports at the top of the engine had fractured. This was unbelievably bad and would possibly mean the end of our rally. Where would we find the parts to repair the engine of a 40-year-old Mercedes-Benz in the wilds of Turkey? I went inside the resort, found one of the Turkish guides who were helping with the rally, and explained I would need to have our car trucked back to Istanbul where I hoped we could repair it. Mark took the news surprisingly well and kept trying to talk me into having some dinner. But I couldn't eat and later couldn't sleep, devastated by the thought that some miscue on my part had destroyed our chances of driving around the world.

Ironically, Innes Ireland's Mercedes-Benz had also blown a head gasket on the 1968 London to Sydney rally. The cause had been a broken radiator and overheating, but Ireland, too, was forced to try to repair his stricken car out in the bush. Unfortunately, his breakdown would ultimately be the cause of his official retirement from the event. I could only hope that we wouldn't share his fate.

The next morning while waiting for the truck that would take our stricken car back to Istanbul, I sought out Carrie Balfour. She and her husband, Will, were driving a fabulous open 1935 Talbot AV 105 Alpine sports car around the world. Their car was my favorite on the event, and Carrie was rapidly becoming one of my best friends. Short in stature with a sort of windswept appearance, Carrie has a sympathetic face that always makes her look like she is about to burst into tears. This gentle appearance notwithstanding, she is tough enough to have decided to drive around the world with her husband in an open pre-War sports car. She and Will had come on the rally looking for adventure, leaving behind two small boys and a farm in Scotland. When I asked them why they had chosen the open and sparse Talbot for the trip, they looked at me like I had come from Mars. "There was never any doubt we would take the Talbot," replied Carrie. "It's the car we do things in." she added confidently. They had owned it for more than 25 years.

Sitting in the morning sun in Bolu, Turkey, with Carrie, I was in low spirits. Mark and I had talked the night before and decided we would try and fix the car in Istanbul and then catch up with the rally before it reached the ferryboat crossing of the Caspian Sea from Azerbaijan. The schedule of this special chartered ferry was fixed, and if we missed it we wouldn't be able to continue. But leaving the rally now meant we would be on our own for boarder crossings in the former Soviet Union and would have to drive day and night to catch up with the others. We had five days until the ferry left, and that didn't seem like much time. What's more, Mark was fearful of driving across these unknown places without the company of the rest of the rally. Remembering the U.S. State Department warnings about travel for American citizens, I knew he had a point; but I also knew I wouldn't quit, even if I had to leapfrog along the rally with other forms of transportation. When I spoke with Carrie I told her my fears and asked her to start trying to find another team that might have an open seat in their car so I could tag along if the worst happened and our U.S. Mercedes Team was unable to continue. She promised she would ask around and as the flatbed truck arrived, I wondered if I would ever see Carrie or any of the others again.

Our Mercedes-Benz was loaded onto a two-level flatbed truck in company with Richard Taylor and David Pierce's 1968 Saab that had eaten its transmission. More precisely, their Saab was beginning to make suspicious noises; and the two Americans from Arizona were shipping it back to Istanbul to see if they could find someone to repair it. Our car went on the bot-

Back to Istanbul after a major engine problem.

tom, and we started on the five-hour truck ride back to Istanbul. Because the cab of the truck would only hold three, and Richard and David were already in the cab, Mark and I rode in our car on the back of the truck. Strapped in with our competition seatbelts and listening to our CD player, we were not only more comfortable than Richard and David, who were jammed into the cab of the truck with the driver, we were probably a lot safer. When we arrived at Mengerler Ticaret Turk Mercedes-Benz, Herr Siegfried Vogt from Germany met us at the shop door as we rolled our stricken Mercedes off the truck. Herr Vogt has 35 years experience with Mercedes-Benz and was the right man to diagnose our problems. He quickly determined that the camshaft had jumped a tooth when the engine started and did a series of checks to ensure there was no severe internal damage. It turned out that, unknown to me and unrecorded in the factory shop manual we were carrying, the hydraulic chain tensioner needs to be removed from the engine and primed with oil before the car is started. I had done everything correctly except this vital step, and it had nearly cost us more than two and a half years of effort! Using a special fiber-optic viewer, Herr Vogt determined that although the valves had hit the pistons

The mechanics at the Mercedes-Benz dealer in Istanbul scrambled to get us back into the rally.

in each of the cylinders, there appeared to be no real internal damage. This was a relief, as locally there were no spare head gaskets available for our engine, and we had used our only spare putting the engine together in Bolu.

Herr Vogt decided to leave the head on the car and simply replace the damaged camshaft supports. He called a local classic Mercedes parts supplier and told them in no uncertain terms to find the parts we needed. I began to feel a bit better and was suddenly grateful that we had chosen to drive a vehicle with such competent worldwide servicing. Although closing time was 6 p.m., Herr Vogt and two of his mechanics stayed late to keep us in the rally. Remarkably, by 8 p.m. the parts were in our hands and by 10:30 p.m. we were back on the road after Siegfried Vogt himself had retuned our carburetors and road tested our vehicle. As he hammered the car through the back streets of Istanbul, he clearly approved of our old car and how we had prepared it. Ahead however, Mark and I faced an all night drive across Turkey to Samsun on the Black Sea where the rest of the rally was spending the night.

It was a tough drive of more than 700 kilometers. The first 400 were

on four-lane highways, but the last 300 were on two-lane roads over mountain passes. Traffic was extremely heavy, but we saw a total of less than
a dozen cars. Heavy trucks and buses own the roads at night in Turkey,
and we spent most of the night dodging the giants. To make matters worse,
Turkish drivers seldom use their headlights, and so lumbering giants would
suddenly appear out of the darkness. The concentration it took to avoid
getting killed was intense. It vied with that narrow road in Greece as
the most dangerous drive of my life. Once again our drive had an eerie
similarity to a section through Turkey driven by the Mercedes team
during the 1968 London to Sydney Rally. "Mikey came to a fastish but
blind right-hander to find a lorry going in the same direction as ourselves,
but completely on the wrong side of the road. As we had a speed differential of something like 60 mph, Mikey just kept going and overtook this
fellow on the inside, hoping he wouldn't suddenly decide to come back
to his correct side of the road. Guesswork played a major part in the early
stages of our journey through Turkey" (Innes Ireland in *Sideways to
Sydney*)

Mark and I were both accomplished long-distance drivers, but at one
stage of our nightmarish drive we were switching off every hour as the
fatigue of the past two days took its toll. The anger I had felt about Mark's
lack of help working on the car in Bolu had evaporated, and I was happy
to have him along to share the danger.

In the 1908 New York to Paris Race, George Schuster and his crew on
the Thomas also had an all-night drive after making repairs. He wrote: "We
drove through the night and the next day, fighting sleep and fatigue. Miller
relieved me at driving but he was equally weary, and I awoke once and
grabbed the wheel just in time to keep the Thomas from going into a ditch.
We arrived in Dvinsk at noon, crossed the Dvina River, rolled south to
Kovno and rested a few hours."

Back in Turkey, shortly after 5:00 A.M., the sky began to lighten as the
sun slowly crept into the sky. We still needed to switch off driving, but at
least we could see the trucks as they careened towards us. We arrived in
Samsun on the Black Sea at 7:30 A.M., less than an hour before we were due
to leave for our next section of the rally. We had missed all of the controls
the day before, except the first one, and added six hours of penalties to our
growing total. But because we checked into that first control at Bolu before
leaving with the tow truck to Istanbul, we avoided an extra 12-hour penalty.
Now we were back and ready to resume the rally.

Later, when I saw Carrie, she smiled and admitted she hadn't even had
a chance to look for a ride for me. Beverly gave me a hug before jumping
into her car with Ed and racing off on the day's run. Several people who
had seen us depart on the truck yesterday came up to say how glad they

were to see us back so soon. It was a warm feeling that these people who were strangers two weeks ago were becoming our friends.

I was feeling decidedly less friendly toward the rally organization. Despite assurances that they wouldn't do so, the organizers had cancelled our hotel rooms in Samsun when we hadn't arrived the night before. I desperately needed a shower and a few minutes rest before facing the day's rallying, but the hotel wouldn't give me a room, claiming I was no longer part of the rally. Finally, after getting nowhere at the front desk, Rich Newman from Chicago, driving the tiny Citroen 2CV in the pre-War category, gave me the keys to his room so that I could at least shower.

We began our drive on time along the coast of the Black Sea. The locals had warned us that truck traffic on the two-lane road would be heavy. Well, we already knew something about Turkish truck traffic. We spent most of the morning dodging local cars and busses and playing chicken with huge trucks as we passed the grossly overloaded vehicles that were blocking our progress. If you judge from its truck traffic, Turkey has a healthy economy.

The world we were traveling through was also becoming more Muslim, with the occasional minaret showing from behind a row of houses. As we drove along the coast we saw several rally cars pulled off on scenic overlooks for lunch, but we didn't think we could spare the time.

The seaside towns of Persembe, Ordu and Pirazaz went by before noon, and we passed through Giresun before finding Tirebolu and a turn away from the coast and inland. In each town hundreds of well wishers were standing by the sides of the road cheering. School children wearing bright blue uniforms lined the route cheering and waving. Often both sides of the road would be filled with smiling faces atop a sea of bright blue. It was like a holiday and a festival rolling down the highway. In larger towns the crowds would press closer to the cars, making it difficult to move forward. It seemed inevitable that when a teenage girl stepped in front of Henning Ulrich's 1960 Mercedes diesel while he was creeping forward he hit her and knocked her down. A policeman picked her up and shook her to show Henning that she was okay and then motioned for him to continue. It was unnerving driving with people pressed against the sides of the car, but the crowds were waving and friendly.

After turning inland, the terrain immediately changed to steep mountains with terraced green hillsides. A wild whitewater river traveled through the bottom of the gorge as we snaked along a brand-new ribbon of highway. We marveled at the huge tunnels that had been blasted into the hillside and the incredible quality of the road to Dogankent and our next time control. It was a beautiful drive, and we appreciated it even in our sleep-deprived state. The grade got steeper, and soon we were driving over a 6,000-foot pass in the Black Sea Mountains. The road here was older than

Near Dogankent, Turkey, just before another timed special section.

the one in the spectacular valley below us. Finally, we reached our time control, high in the mountains for a special timed section.

The section covered a goat track for 16.6-kilometers (10.3-miles) over
a mountain ridge between Dogankent and Zigani Gecidi. We were allowed
thirteen minutes for the section. It was a horribly rough road with boulders, dirt and gravel, hairpin turns and hundred foot drop-offs. Neither
Mark nor I had slept in more than 30 hours, and my goal was simply to get
both the car and us through the section in one piece. Mark hates rallying
in the mountains and was visibly nervous. I was just tired. My eyes felt
gritty in the bright sunlight, and I wanted nothing more than a hotel bed
to sleep in. The day's finish and that hotel bed, however, were on the other
side of the special timed section. The section was difficult to drive, and it
was impossible to stay on time. The best team was the Japanese 1965 Datsun 410 with a professional rally driver who managed it in 7 minutes over
the target. Exhausted as I was, and unwilling to make any mistakes, I took
a leisurely 10 minutes over target time and was happy to have survived the
day intact. Although the human crew members were exhausted, our hearty
old Mercedes-Benz, after running continuously for more than 19 hours
since the repairs in Istanbul, seemed to be fine.

Fortunately, the Zorlu Grand Hotel in Trabzon was modern and elegant — with leather chairs, stained glass windows and a huge marble staircase. Parking was in the crowded basement, and it took half an hour to get the car jammed into its spot. Mark and I joined Henning and Klemens to walk to a nearby Chinese restaurant. I was so tired I could barely see the menu and declined when Henning suggested we hit some of Trabzon's nightspots. It never occurred to me to ask how Henning knew of nightspots in Trabzon. Mark took him up on it, and they went off drinking. I crawled into bed shortly after 7 p.m. and, just before I fell asleep, I remembered that our next day's route would take us into the countries that used to form part of what Ronald Reagan once referred to as the Evil Empire of the Soviet Union.

6

The Place We Dreaded to Go

"I could not in good conscience today call the Soviet Union an evil empire."
— Ronald Reagan, 1989

From the beginning, everyone knew that the Republics that made up the former Soviet Union would be the wild cards in this event. Tales abounded of difficult travel conditions, corrupt public officials and substandard medical facilities across the southern part of our former cold-war enemy. We would be entering another world, and once inside it wasn't exactly clear how we could get out if everything went to hell.

Mark and I also had some realities to face, and I called a team meeting as we loaded our gear into the car. The engine had performed well in our overnight drive from Istanbul and subsequent day of driving along the Black Sea, but we had no assurance that we hadn't warped the cylinder head or damaged the valves with our earlier problems. On top of that, we had used our spare cylinder head gasket, and it would be next to impossible to find another until we reached North America. Before that, we had to cross the former Soviet Republics and all of China with its fearsome deserts. It was a long way to go without a safety net. We would be entering the most remote and difficult part of the journey knowing we would have to baby our machine to make sure it would survive. As much as we might want to trust the old beast, there was a fair chance the car would leave us stranded.

Then there was the competitive aspect of the event. After losing an hour in our crash in Greece, we had adopted a strategy of holding back and waiting for the leaders to have problems and come back to us. Now, with an additional five hours of penalty from missing a day's controls, we knew we would have to be lucky to get a top ten finish. This was a real shame.

Crossing the border into Georgia.

Peter Banham, one of the event mechanics, had confided to me that he and his fellow mechanics had been impressed with our level of preparation and had predicted a top five finish for our team. Well, that was out the window. Fred Giles was still leading in his Hillman Hunter with just a few minutes of penalty, a remarkable achievement. Mark and I talked about it, but our path was clear. Before the event we had agreed that we would do whatever it took to finish, no matter how far down in the standings we dropped. As much as we hated to admit it, finishing, not placing, was now the goal.

After such long delays at the Turkish border crossing, we anticipated that our arrival into Georgia would be worse. We had been allotted five hours for the crossing by an obviously nervous organizing team. The Georgians turned out to be friendly and accommodating to the rally, the first international motorsport event ever to enter their country. The border crossing took less than an hour, and we arrived for our overnight stop in the town of Batumi, Georgia, on the Black Sea coast in the early afternoon.

It was immediately clear that Georgia was different from Turkey. The people were much more somber, and in towns only the children would wave. The adults have good reason to be somber. The Russians ravaged their country when they pulled out after the fall of communism. They took everything of value and were determined to destroy much of what they couldn't take. Irrigation systems lay shattered and rusting in the fields. The electric transmission towers were still in place, but almost all of the electric wires had been removed, stolen for the value of their copper wire. The fields were planted with only enough crops to support the local area; and unlike Turkey, there was almost no truck traffic. Trucks are a good indicator of the viability of the economy, and by this standard the Republic of Georgia was in deep trouble. The fields were fenced; not to keep the animals in, but rather to keep the livestock off of them. Cows, goats, pigs and sheep wandered freely on the roads, feeding on whatever they could find on the grass verges. The roads were in terrible shape. They had once been paved; but there was no money to keep them from deteriorating; and there were huge potholes everywhere. In the countryside everyone waved, and the atmosphere seemed much more relaxed. Young men rode beautiful horses, obviously a symbol of status in this place. I wondered if a 16-year-old Georgian male would rather own a horse or a used Lada automobile?

Batumi is an old Soviet resort town that used to be a favorite destination for Russian tourists. They don't come anymore, and the large Intourist

Rush hour on a Georgian highway.

Hotel on the Black Sea was filled to capacity by teams from the rally. A second hotel, the Sputnik, handled the overflow. People who stayed there were able to tell horror stories about the place for the rest of the rally. Many of the hotels in the area were filled with refugees from the conflict in Abkhazian, an area in South Georgia that was intent on its independence. People caught in the middle of the conflict fled by the thousands to Batumi and other cities to get away from the fighting.

In the car park, hundreds of children wanted to see the cars, and many received small presents or photographs of the cars from the competitors. It was quite a sight to see pretty American Kelly Secrest (a police officer in real life), surrounded by children three ranks deep, all wanting to see what presents she might have brought for them. Many of the competitors had made postcards of their cars to hand out while others had pens or pencils to give away. The kids had to compete with security officers who would shoo the children away and then ask for pens and postcards for themselves. Still, everyone seemed happy to see us, and lovely Georgian girls flirted with the rally drivers.

The Intourist Hotel was like a faded dowager. It had beautiful chandeliers and ceilings, but the atmosphere was cold and remote. The place

Kelly Secrest entertains the locals in Batumi, Georgia.

had the distinctive smell of coal heat and old lead-base paint mixed with decades of dust that so many Soviet-era buildings seem to cultivate. On each level sat an old peasant woman, wrapped in a shawl and kerchief, who acted as hall monitor, in charge of all that happened on her floor. Predictably, the elevators were slow and unreliable, and it was faster to run up a few flights of deeply worn marble stairs. In the evening, we were entertained at a lavish dinner with the appropriate dignitaries and officials. The tables were set in the grand ballroom, which bore signs of having once been quite impressive, and it was clear that the Georgians looked upon us as people of major importance. The President of Adjaria, the autonomous region of The Republic of Georgia, arrived, and everyone stood as he walked to the head table. Like people everywhere in the world, Georgians are proud of their children, and young dancers and singers made the dinner memorable. The singers performed modern songs and traditional Georgian ballads. Toward the end of the evening, a group of large men who had been sitting somewhat ominously in the upper balcony stood and began to sing. Their voices were deep and perfectly harmonized and they sang without accompaniment. It was extraordinary. It was clear that our rally was really important to these people, a chance for them to show that they, too, have something to offer the world.

Later, we learned that the event was videotaped and televised, used by "His Excellency" the president to show how he was making his region an important part of the former Soviet world. Apparently, he had the reputation of being the local bully and was trying to use us to help soften his image. Several of the all-male teams also reported that after retiring for the evening, the old crones in charge of each floor made it clear that they could procure prostitutes. Amazing what can be communicated, even when nobody speaks the other's language. Nobody knocked on our door to offer their services, but apparently we were in a minority.

From Batumi, we continued the next day on to Tiblisi over fairly rough roads. Large potholes and washouts were common, and I had to take great care to avoid impacts that could break the suspension or bend a wheel. Cows, pigs and goats wandered freely, adding to the hazards; and two lane roads were frequently used for three lanes of traffic, as passing in Georgia is considered a contact sport.

As we drove, I remembered a story that Mario Andretti told of being a small boy and watching the racing cars in the Mille Miglia pass through his village when he was growing up in Italy. He said that seeing the cars flash by had produced the desire to become a racing driver, and he ultimately won the Indy 500 and became a Formula 1 world champion. In the same way, five-time world driving champion Juan Manuel Fangio talked about seeing racing cars roaring through his village during South American road races when he was a child. In the back of my mind, I hoped that against all the odds, our drive through these villages might somehow inspire a child in the same way. Who knows, maybe in a dozen or so years a new driving champion will emerge from rural Georgia?

Along the way, we passed the city of Gori, the birthplace of Joseph Stalin. As bad as things are in the former Soviet Union, they had to have been worse under the tyrant who would execute his own army officers for fear of their disloyalty. We were told by the locals that one reason that the Russians destroyed so much when they pulled out was due to their hatred of the Georgians and of Stalin. We think of the Soviet Union as having been one large menacing homogeneous force, but the truth is that it was made up of numerous regions and peoples, each with their own customs, opinions, biases and hatreds. With the fall of the unifying Soviet government, those hatreds are now free to come to the surface, and the rape of Georgia was one result.

Arriving in Tiblisi, we found the completely modern Sheraton Matechti Palace Hotel waiting for us. Modern, except for the presence of an unopened bottle of water next to the tap for brushing teeth. It was a not-so-subtle reminder that we were now in a part of the world where it wasn't safe to drink the water.

The Sheraton sits on a hillside overlooking Tiblisi, a city of over a million. A river runs through the city, and there are wide streets and tree-lined boulevards adding to the beauty. Despite its pleasant layout, the results of a civil war in the early 1990s were all too apparent with empty buildings and hotels surrounding the downtown. Fighting took place within the city limits; and, as in the rest of Georgia, it is difficult to understand how the people of Tiblisi will ever get back on their feet again.

During the day off in Tiblisi, we worked on the car and did our laundry. Mark was typically in charge of making sure our clothes got clean on our days off, and he did so either through the hotel, or by finding a laundromat somewhere in the city. With all of the weight for spare parts and other necessities that we were carrying, we had agreed that our personal gear should be as light as possible. This meant if we wore most things twice, each of us only had at most about a week's worth of clean clothes; and a day off meant making sure we'd be ready for the upcoming week. Once again, much of my day was spent on journalistic commitments. I was amazed that Internet access from the hotels in the former Soviet Republics wasn't proving to be a problem. Using my laptop and images from my Nikon digital camera, I was able to file stories and reports complete with on the scene color photography.

Late in the afternoon, Mark and I joined many of the rally teams on a brief bus tour of the city which ended at a shop selling Persian rugs. After

Descendents of rug merchants in Tiblisi who probably sold their wares to Marco Polo.

being cooped up in a car for day after day, some of the rallyist couldn't restrain themselves and went on a shopping spree. The rug merchants, who could no doubt trace their ancestors back to merchants who sold Persian rugs to Marco Polo, were happy to arrange shipment of the purchases to anywhere in the world. While it was nice to finally see some of the world (aside from car repair shops), neither Mark nor I were overcome by any such shopping urges.

The next morning found us headed to the Caspian Sea for an appointment with a specially chartered ferry that would take us from Azerbaijan across the inland sea to Turkmenistan. Our route book said, "Please be aware if you are not on the ferry this evening the rally moves on without you." This was real incentive, and some of the older cars left early, taking a penalty but ensuring that they would reach the ferry in plenty of time. After a short drive across the remainder of Georgia, we arrived at the border with Azerbaijan where the customs and border guards met us with warmth and enthusiasm. Local residents in Azerbaijan, too, seemed to be much more cheerful and happy than their Georgian neighbors. The high-

Azerbaijan has a vastly better infrastructure than its Georgian neighbors.

way was in reasonable condition, and truck and bus traffic was evident. The terrain was mostly rolling hills and lush green trees. Our route took us south along the southernmost end of the Caucasus Mountains. Eventually we turned east and crossed over several passes. Flocks of goats and sheep were everywhere, and occasionally a skinned goat was hung from a stick at the side of the road as an invitation for Azerbaijani fast food. I wondered what his fellow goats thought of this form of advertising.

Carrie and Will Balfour in the prewar Talbot had stopped by the roadside for some minor repair. A herd of animals was nearby, tended by shepherds.

Carrie said to Will, "I wonder if these are sheep or goats?"

One of the grizzled shepherds smiled at her and replied in perfect English, "They are sheep."

Concerned with making the ferry on time, we passed on local gastronomic opportunities as Mark munched on a couple of NutriBiotic bars, and I hoped that we might find food on the ferry. I had discovered that Mark's favorite energy food bars, of which we had packed several hundred, tasted terrible. What's more, they gave me the runs, and so I was avoiding them. They didn't seem to affect Mark, and he could enjoyably pack away three or four at a sitting. We hadn't spoken much since that long drive across Turkey, and we both knew that this trial by fire had solidified our team. Mark went out drinking every night with some of the other Americans, while I tinkered on the car or tried to get to know some of the people on the other teams. There was little tension but no real conversation in our car as we headed into Baku. Maybe my daughter was right. Maybe we had already run out of things to talk about.

Our route instructions took us to the "Motodrom" where we would wait for two hours before we were led by police convoy to the port to board the ferry. The Motodrom is a kart and motorcycle racing track, and its parking lot was hot and dusty and filled with people who had come to see what this event was all about. Slick young men in suits with cell phones driving expensive cars were perfect caricatures of the Soviet Mafia we had heard so much about. Organized crime is a big deal here, as Azerbaijan has vast amounts of natural gas to help fuel its economy. There were a variety of cars, mostly older Soviet-built Ladas, but also many newer Mercedes-Benz and BMW sedans. Many were painted black and slightly sinister.

It is a curious thing to travel by car across Asia. You see a transition in people and culture at almost the perfect pace. People who live here don't travel much, and if they do it's by bus, train or horse. In general, this means a person from a village only meets and marries a person from another nearby village. If you were to travel by horse across the countryside, let's say 30 to 40 miles a day, the change in the people would be so slow you would miss it. If you were to fly from major city to major city, the abrupt differences would be too great. But travel 300–400 miles per day in a car, and you can see the gradual change in people and their culture as you drive from west to east. To the west, people appear European. While driving eastward the influence of the Mongols gradually becomes more evident in their genetic makeup. Eventually, the Chinese influence begins to surface. The same is true for the architecture and the artwork that one sees, but the key is that you have to travel at the right pace to see the changes. Our battered old Mercedes was keeping us at that pace.

Finally, after eating melting ice cream bars and standing around in the heat, it was our time to leave the Motordrom in a convoy. We followed a speeding police escort through a maze of streets to the ferry docks on the Caspian Sea. The drive seemed to take forever, and we later found out that the police had led us through their favorite neighborhoods to show us off before finally bringing us to the ferry docks. After another long wait, we were allowed to load our cars onto the *Dagestan*, a decrepit ferryboat chartered by the organizers just for this event. The ship was old and tired although a coat of new paint had been recently splashed over its rusting

Will and Carrie Balfour drive their 1934 Talbot onto the decrepit vessel *Dagestan.*

decks to give an illusion of seaworthiness. About a third of the rally participants got cabins, the rest were left to sleeping on airplane-style seats or on the floor. Mark and I felt like lottery winners when we found that we had been assigned to a two-man cabin with a working flush toilet. We even had a porthole. On the horizon and all around the port of Baku were huge oil and natural gas derricks, pumping out the money that is the only thing separating the prosperity of Azerbaijan and her people from the plight that the Georgians face.

In Baku, Klemens Suchocki was forced to leave the rally. In France he had left his jacket at a hotel and in one of its pockets was his passport. Henning contacted the hotel; and they promised to send the jacket to Istanbul; but when we arrived, there was no jacket. Klemens spoke fluent Russian and was able to bluff his way through Georgia and Azerbaijan, but the chances of making it into China were slim. Although Klemens hadn't been much help as a mechanic when it came to my engine problems, he was a likable guy and seemed like a part of the family. He flew back to Europe; and Terry Maxon, who was the driver of Car #2, the big yellow 1913 Rolls Royce that had finally retired in Istanbul, signed on as Henning's navigator. Terry had been bumming rides until this point because he wanted to be a part of the event and not fly home to California. He promised Henning that he was an expert mechanic, spoke Russian and Chinese fluently and didn't snore. It's amazing what people will say just to stay in a rally.

The *Dagestan* was supposed to make the trip across the Caspian Sea to Turkmenibashi in about 14 hours. Shortly after leaving port, the captain shut down one of the two engines to save expensive fuel, and we worked our way across the oily smooth waters in about 18 hours. Life on-board was not as desperate as we were led to believe it would be. These were not luxury accommodations, but the *Dagestan* was no charter yacht. During more prosperous times she carried railroad cars across the Caspian. Now she carries anything for anyone with hard currency to spend. I set about exploring the vessel, but after finding a flooded passageway below decks, decided that there were things I didn't want to know about the *Dagestan*. Coming back onto the deck I ran into a crew member who, although he spoke no English, managed to convey to me that he wanted to rent me his cabin. He showed me his luxurious accommodations, complete with lavish pornographic images cut from magazines taped to the walls. I praised the work of his decorator but told him that I already had a cabin. Those without our deluxe accommodations had to sleep sitting up and contend with badly overflowing toilets, and I am pretty sure that the sailor eventually found someone among the passengers to rent his cabin. The food on the ship matched the overall décor and decrepitude, and Mark and I decided to pass on dinner. Others, especially those who were celebrating French competitor Claude Picasso's birthday, suffered the next day from the gastronomic experience.

Upon our arrival at the port of Turkmenibashi, we encountered another delay. Despite months of planning and local representation, the immigration and customs officials seemed to know nothing about the rally. On top of that, the woman who was supposed to spray insecticide on the tires of each vehicle had just gone to lunch. Three hours passed before the middle-aged uniformed functionary returned from her midday meal, and the first cars were released. By the time we were processed through the port it was past 5 P.M. and we still had more than 300 miles of driving across the desert ahead of us.

The drive across the desert introduced us to a new hazard, one that we would eventually become used to in our drive across Asia. Camels would wander across the road, often materializing magically from a dip near the edge of the roadway. As night fell, the light-colored surface of the narrow two-lane paved road became difficult to distinguish from the edges of the desert, making a long drive even tougher. Shortly after dusk, we ran into swarms of black bugs that smashed themselves onto the windshield,

Our first encounter with camels came after arriving into Turkmenistan by ferry boat.

rendering it nearly opaque. Everyone was forced to stop and clean off the bugs that defied every attempt at removal using the windshield wipers and washers.

Unlike drivers in Turkey who eschewed any lights at all, drivers in Turkmenistan drive with their high beams blazing all the time, mindless of the blinding effect it has on oncoming traffic. We flashed our super-bright driving lights at the trucks and buses, but were unable to change their native behavior. When we stopped for gas, the car was immediately engulfed by groups of children, wanting a pen or photograph of the car as a souvenir of our passage. We had printed 400 postcards with our car and team name on them, but we were rapidly running out. Mark held the crowds at bay while I filled the gas tank. We arrived a bit past 1 A.M. in the capital city of Ashgabad, happy to have made the distance without incident aside from getting lost as we tried to follow the once-again obscure directions to our hotel.

After all the trouble getting into Turkmenistan, our stay in Ashgabad was pleasant and the people quite extraordinary. As explained to me by one of the locals, the Soviet Union decided it needed to populate the region after World War II and sent people from all over its empire to live in

Ashgabad. Normally, this would be a recipe for ethnic strife and perhaps war, but for some reason the people mixed well together and the result is a satisfying mixture of east and west. One thing that didn't need explaining to me was how the women of Ashgabad benefited from the widely varied gene pool that came from centuries of east and west trading. They are exceptionally beautiful. This was not just my opinion. Marco Polo in the 13th Century described the mixed lineage of the North Persians as "a handsome race, especially the women, who, in my opinion, are the most beautiful in the world." I agreed with Mr. Polo. Turkmenistan is newly independent (1991), and the capital is quite modern, thanks to a benevolent president (for life) and lots of oil and gas money. The people were extremely friendly and seemed happy to be living in their city of a half million.

We spent most of our day off in Ashgabad checking over the car, and I took a taxi to the Mercedes-Benz dealer to find a spare set of brake pads. I asked about a spare cylinder head gasket, but none was available for a car built 40 years earlier. Predictably the service bays were filled with other competitors' Mercedes-Benz cars being serviced. Most of the repairs appeared fairly minor: broken shock absorbers and fractured brackets from the pounding the cars had taken. The Bush family from Germany, whose 1956 Mercedes 190 model appeared to be perfectly stock down to its hubcaps, had a broken generator bracket that needed a repair; but to get to it, the mechanics at the service center had to disassemble half of the front of the engine. Ashgabad also spelled the end of the road for the Mercedes-Benz Coupe from Argentina that had hit us in Greece. Ominously, they blew a head gasket, and no spares were available. They had studiously avoided me ever since the accident, and I can't say I blamed them. I still felt pretty guilty about involving them in the crash, especially whenever I saw their crushed fender, still held together by the roadside bungy cord repair that Mark and I had effected. I was also avoiding the couple in the dark blue Jaguar, whom I still partly blamed for our accident. It was normal for cliques to form as we continued eastward, and there were a few of the London to Beijing competitors whom I never really got to know.

While I was hobnobbing with the gentry at the Mercedes-Benz dealer, others were discovering the delights that Ashgabad had to offer. Ed and Beverly took a tour of the city that included a stop at a new shopping mall. They described the multi-level attraction complete with a three-story waterfall as magnificent. They also said that all of the stores within the complex were completely devoid of merchandise. Later, they saw a huge golden statue of President Saparmurat Niyazov. The statue sits on a revolving turntable timed so that the president's golden face is always pointed toward the sun. The president's face also adorns the money and stamps and can be

Entering the Garagum Desert in Turkmenistan.

seen everywhere in the city. Strangely, each portrait of the president depicts him at a different stage in his life, so in some he is a strapping dark haired young man, while in others he is a wise-looking white haired elder. One thing that everyone could agree on: it's good to be king.

We left Ashgabad the next day and immediately entered the southern Garagum (Black Sand) Desert. Temperatures were in the upper 80's with a relentless sun, and it made driving in the open cars hot work. Our car was hot but not unbearable inside, and we drank plenty of bottled water to keep dehydration at bay. At one point the route passed within five kilometers of Iran but the map was straightforward, and we avoided any unplanned border crossings. We had pushed our fuel mileage on this section, covering more than 600 kilometers (370 miles) on a tank, but finally had to fill up at a station that only served 76-octane gasoline. We had stupidly passed by several stations earlier that carried high-octane fuel, and now we couldn't afford to be choosy. For once we were thankful that while preparing for the rally we had lowered the compression ratio of our engine to cope with just such a circumstance. On the other hand, Ed and Bev Suhrbier filled up their Mercedes-Benz Cabriolet at a modern high-octane station just outside Ashgabad and immediately had car problems. The tank of fuel they received had lots of water in it, and they had earlier given up on their water-separating filter after it caused them problems. They struggled along until they found good fuel in the desert town of Mary.

Mary (also called Merv) is a pleasant if somewhat dusty small town in the Garagum Desert in Turkmenistan. It was founded in 330 BC by Alexander the Great and grew large and prosperous, becoming a major trading center on the Silk Road to China. The ruins from these early times can still be seen on the banks of the river. Early in the 13th century it was conquered and became a part of Ghengis Khan's empire. When a representative of Khan's far flung empire arrived to collect taxes, the townspeople decided not to pay and murdered the taxman. Khan's son sent an army of 100,000 soldiers to Mary, and in one night they murdered a million people in retaliation. Each soldier was responsible for killing 10 townspeople. Maybe it was just my imagination working overtime, but there was a stillness in Mary that I have also felt in places like the battlefield in Gettysburg and at the Great Lakes Shipwreck Museum on Whitefish Point in Michigan, not far from where the Edmund Fitzgerald sank. I found it vaguely eerie and was happy to put Mary behind us.

The Bayramaly Region of Turkmenistan is known for its strict religious practices. As far as we were concerned, it was also known for groups of boys who threw rocks at passing rally cars. Several times we were pelted as we went by, the rocks bouncing off the sides of our car. Ed and Beverly of Team Suhrbier weren't so lucky. One rock put a fist-sized hole in their Mercedes windshield while another shattered the side window next to Beverly. If she had been riding with the window open as she usually did, she might have been badly injured. Suddenly the groups of smiling and waving children on the sides of the roads seemed like a menace rather than an occasion. Others also had cracked windshields and dented fenders from the rock throwers.

Arriving in Chardzhou we were directed to the Sanatoriy Profilaktorisi, which would be our "hotel" for the evening. Rumors abounded that this place was once a tuberculosis hospital that had been converted to other uses. The rooms were sparse, containing only a couple of hard wooden beds and plastic chairs. The door to the bathroom in each room was firmly nailed shut, and the entire rally was directed to use one bathroom with three toilet stalls. At least they were flush toilets—until they became stopped up. Beyond these charms, there was live entertainment that evening under the stars in the form of a band and singers. The bar encouraged us, through the magic of alcohol, to forget the day's drive and the abysmal surroundings. Russian beer is strong and comes in industrial size bottles. It is said that it was also once fortified with formaldehyde, but this practice has now ended. At least that was the official position. Mark proclaimed it drinkable. I thought I could detect the faint flavor of chemicals... Dinner was served, and although it was hot, much of it was also unidentifiable. We felt bad about not eating everything that was offered, especially in a country where food isn't plentiful, but the risk of stomach problems when we needed to be on the move each day made most people extra cautious. In fact, most of the rallyists seated at one table at the sanatorium dinner ended up suffering for several days after eating all that was offered.

The evening started out pleasantly enough, and the female singer had a nice voice. Unfortunately for exhausted rally competitors, the loud band and singer insisted on performing late into the night, even after all of the paying customers had gone to their rooms and were trying to sleep. Popping a sleeping pill helped. It was the kind of miserable and mind-numbing experience that you later realize was one of the reasons you came on this adventure in the first place. Besides, from then on whenever anyone said "the Sanatorium" you immediately knew what they meant. The shared experiences, good and bad, were molding even the most anti-social of us into a disaffected group rather than a bunch of disaffected individuals.

The next day's border crossing into Uzbekistan was one that everyone dreaded. Uzbekistan had held all of our passports until several days before the rally started, trying to decide whether or not to let us in. More likely they were looking for some additional grease from Philip Young. We had expected the worst that a third world country could throw at us, so it was a genuine shock when we found that the border guards were ready with smiles and lists, and the border was easy to cross. Soon we were driving along a four-lane divided highway across the Karsi Steppe on our way to the legendary city of Samarkand. Temperatures were in the low 90s, and I drank more than three liters of water over a six-hour period. I am not sure how teams like Carrie and Will Balfour in their open Talbot managed to survive the heat. Upon arriving in Samarkand, we were directed by police and military units off of the rally route. As our directions into cities and to hotels had been so bad up to that point, we weren't too worried about the deviation from the prescribed course. We eventually ended up at the airport where we all parked in a large fenced lot with armed guards. We were happy to see a beat-up old fuel tank truck waiting for us with what we were told was 90-octane gasoline. We were in no position to be choosy as the guards made it clear once our cars were in their parking lot, they weren't going to let them back out. Eventually, a bus took us to a Soviet-style hotel in the middle of the museum district of the city.

Our fears about Uzbekistan were not entirely unfounded. The U.S. State Department warned, "American citizens are urged to be aware of an increased threat of terrorist violence in Uzbekistan and the heightened

Approaching the border with Uzbekistan.

activity and vigilance by the security forces responding to that threat. This heightened security stance is in response to fighting on the Tajikistan-Kyrgyzstan and Tajikistan-Uzbekistan borders, which has included recent hostage-taking incidents in Kyrgyzstan directly targeted against foreign citizens, one of which involved American citizens. American citizens are urged to avoid all travel in these regions." This was, of course, precisely the area into which we were heading. Chris Jensen's advice to purchase kidnapping insurance seemed sound. The State Department warnings also included: "Some areas of Uzbekistan, generally on the borders with Tajikistan, Kyrgyzstan and Kazakhstan, have been closed to civilians and tourists due to operations by government security forces. Restricted personal movement, including the closing of roads to traffic and frequent document, vehicle and personal identification checks should be anticipated." I checked the map. Yes, that was where we were going.

That evening, I went to dinner with Carrie and Will Balfour. We found an out of the way Russian restaurant where we were the only English-speakers, and we sat outdoors enjoying the warm evening. Carrie and Will both had goulash, which they said was excellent, and I enjoyed braised lamb chops. Between the company and the delicious food, it was the nicest dinner I had enjoyed in almost a month. When we arrived back at our hotel, the taxi driver refused payment, telling us that our waitress, an attractive blond Russian woman, felt like we had given her too much money for a tip and had paid for our cab fare. Was this the Uzbekistan that we had all feared?

The fenced compound at the airport where the cars were held was heavily guarded by soldiers and police. I arrived early the next morning and began checking over the Mercedes. Modern cars have made routine maintenance almost unnecessary, but old cars require constant attention. Fittings must be greased, ignition timing confirmed, and filters checked and changed on a regular schedule. The constant pounding our cars were being subjected to also made a check of the tightness of nuts and bolts mandatory so that nothing would fall off. Our battered old Mercedes-Benz was holding up well, especially given how it had been abused. Personally I kept waiting for the other shoe to drop. Maybe we had avoided total calamity in our engine repair, but in the back of my mind I knew that if the head gasket were to fail again, our rally would be over.

As I worked on my car, I noticed a small boy of 8 to 10 years old standing along the chain link fence, watching me. After a short time, he climbed

Refueling arrangements in Samarkand.

The security compound at the Samarkand airport.

up and over the fence and sat quietly on the curb, a short distance from my car. I smiled at him, and he shyly smiled back. It was a sunny and glorious morning, and he seemed happy to just sit and watch this strange large man work on an automobile. Unfortunately, a jeep load of security police soon arrived. They called the young boy over to their truck. For 20 minutes they questioned him, sometimes yelling at him and occasionally grabbing his little finger and twisting it. His tormentors were young too, not much more than twenty. He never cried out, even though he was obviously in pain.

I felt helpless and angry. This was not my country, and these were not my customs. What right did I have to interfere? The boy had clearly broken the rules by climbing the fence, yet had he really done anything so wrong? What should I do? Finally, they told him to go and he headed for the fence and began climbing over it. They yelled at him again; and he stopped, meekly climbed down, and walked toward them, holding out the little finger on his right hand so that they could inflict more torture. It broke my heart. They ignored his outstretched hand, and told him to leave by the front gate. All the rest of the morning, many young boys stood outside the fence watching us work and trying out their English on us. None ventured over the fence. The guard's methods were clearly effective, but that small boy paid the price for our security. I wasn't very proud of myself.

Later in the morning, I received an education in Samarkand economy and free market in action. Three teenaged boys had been allowed to set up a car wash area in the car park where we were working. For the first and second car they washed, they charged two U.S. dollars. The third car they charged three. The next car they charged four. Our car was the fifth car they washed, and they charged me five dollars. They tried for six on the next, but the Swedish owner of the Volvo refused to pay it and they settled on four. As the day wore on the price hovered around four until finally the last car they washed they did for two dollars. Even if I had paid at the high end for the washing service, I was happy to be a part of this minor experiment in capitalism.

When I finished my work on the car, I wanted to head back to the hotel. Rally leader Fred Giles also wanted to go back, and we agreed to share a cab. Fred isn't very tall and has a happy disposition and a ready smile. I had heard that he was well-known in vintage racing circles in England and Europe, and the way he was handling the little Hillman Hunter sedan certainly indicated real driving talent. We found a car whose driver said he

The Irish team works on their Mustang in Samarkand.

would take us to the hotel. Shortly after starting out, however, we were flagged down by a police car. Apparently, the car we were riding in wasn't a taxi at all, and the police officers were coming down hard on the driver for offering to drive us for money. It was hot sitting in the car, and eventually Fred and I got out and stood by the side of the road as the cops yelled at our driver. It was hard to follow exactly what was going on, but after awhile one of the cops told us in broken English that we were okay and that they weren't going to arrest us but that our driver was in trouble. Then suddenly, they tired of the game and let us continue on our way with our driver. Fred was pretty angry by now and when we got to the hotel, he refused to pay the fake taxi driver. Fred stalked away toward the hotel, and I stuffed a couple of dollars in the hand of the driver, far less than he was asking for, but probably far better than a stay in a Samarkand jail.

Many people from the rally visited the legendary markets of Samarkand and Registan Square. Trading has taken place here for more than a thousand years. At one time Samarkand was a major stop on the Silk Road and one of the centers of civilization. Bright colors, fabrics, exotic spices, and bins of fruits and nuts were all on display. In my own case most of my afternoon was dedicated to writing stories for the web sites and for Chris Jensen at the *Cleveland Plain Dealer*. This was becoming a real chore, often taking three or four hours of what was supposed to be a rest day. It also seemed somewhat counter to what I should be doing. I was supposed to be reporting about the things I had seen and the places I had visited, and yet the time and effort it took to write about them prevented me from seeing and visiting them. Still, the promises of coverage that I had made had helped to get me on the trip, so I couldn't really complain. Mark went sightseeing although he said the tour wasn't good. Late in the afternoon, I was able to access the Internet from the hotel and sent my stories and some digital photographs back to the States.

The next morning we headed across Uzbekistan toward a night stop in the city of Tashkent, another legendary city along the Silk Road described by Marco Polo. Before arriving there we had to complete a special timed section through the farmlands and small villages far from the main roadway. Ed and Bev had more problems with their brakes and decided to bypass this section by staying on the main road. They figured they had so many penalty points already that a few more weren't going to matter. Several of the pre-War cars took the same option, taking a penalty rather than subjecting their cars to more pounding and abuse.

The section started out through a valley filled with wildflowers. At first the road surface was good, a mixture of smooth gravel with some patched pavement. Even driving carefully we caught up with a few of the rally cars in front of us, although they seemed reluctant to let us pass. As we entered the first village, the road surface quickly deteriorated with deep car-consuming potholes and broken pavement. The crowd in the village was huge. Standing three and four deep, they lined the entire route through town. There were armed police and soldiers everywhere, holding the crowds back from the roadway, but there simply weren't enough to keep children from darting back and forth in front of the cars. One small mistake from a driver and a rally car would mow down dozens of spectators. It was scary and yet exciting. The crowd was cheering and throwing green leafy branches and flowers at the cars. We crept through the crowd and then tried to make up time before coming to another village. The car was going well on these rough roads, even if we were babying the engine. Toward the last part of the special section, there was a long downhill stretch through several canyons with wide sweeping bends. The pavement here was very good, and it was possible to make back most of the time we had lost by going slowly through the villages. By the end of the day's drive we had gained two places in the overall standings, having passed a total of a half dozen cars on this section. This put us someplace in the mid-twenties overall, and Mark and I were re-energized.

Not all cars survived this section entirely intact. Henning and his new navigator Terry hit a huge bump in their diesel Mercedes, putting a hole in its oil pan. As they worked to repair this damage to the car by the side of the road, several of their bags were stolen from the trunk. The bags included cameras, medicine, some personal items and around $300 in cash. They didn't notice the theft until they were underway but later reported it to the police with little hope that their items would ever be seen again. The section was hard on other Mercedes-Benz runners, too, as Brian Rhatigan from Ireland, driving with his son in a Mercedes Coupe like the one we had wanted to bring, hit a pothole while sliding sideways, bending a rear axle shaft and breaking the axle casing. Brian was another one of the rally's real characters. He was late middle aged with a ruddy Irish complexion and a shock of grey hair. Like several others on the rally, Brian had arranged for a succession of co-drivers during the event, including his son, the mechanic who had built the car and a young woman who was his significant other. It meant that throughout the event there would occasionally be new faces and new names to learn. Brian and his son were able to limp their car with its bent axle to the finish and then on to Tashkent where they had to cool their heels the next day at the local Mercedes garage and at a welding shop while the car was repaired. The pair then drove all night to catch back up with the rally.

Later that evening in the hotel restaurant in Tashkent, I saw Don Sevart sitting alone at a table. Don, a tall American from California who looks like an aging surfer-dude, sells classic cars for a living. He had sold Helmut

Karbe the 1929 Bentley Speed Six that the pair were driving in the event. I hadn't spoken much with Don until that point, but he looked so sad that I had to ask him what was wrong. He told me that he and Karbe had been driving through one of the crowded villages when a small boy about six years old darted in front of their car to retrieve some flowers that had been thrown there by some older boys. The left front fender of the car struck the boy in the head and sent him flying across the road. Karbe screeched the Bentley to a stop. Don said there was a lot of blood. Instantly, two large black sedans filled with large men appeared. They kept the crowd away from the Bentley. A screaming woman broke from the crowd and scooped up the small child and carried him to one of the cars. Meanwhile, a huge Army helicopter appeared overhead and hovered over the crowd. The police told Don and Helmut that the child was fine and that they would be giving them a police escort to the hotel. When Don arrived at the hotel, the police told him the boy was fine, just had a bump on the head and was already at home. Don didn't think the child was fine. He was pretty certain that the impact had killed him. He was also certain that he would never know for sure. He was also dismayed that his driver, a rich German, didn't seem at all affected by the tragedy. Don was tired and not feeling well and wanted to go home. I didn't blame him for feeling that way.

The official word spreading around the rally hotel was that the helicopter had airlifted the injured child to a hospital. Don knew that this wasn't true. He figured that the helicopter was there to watch over us, sitting back just far enough to be out of sight but able to make sure that nothing interfered with the rally. Our rich-man's game had become a political event in the control of the governments of each of the countries we were passing through. Each night, regional television would carry coverage of the event, and each country was ensuring that no bad news was reported.

I asked Philip Young the next morning if he had any comment on the incident where the child was killed.

He looked panicked for an instant and he quickly said, "You can't report that! We don't talk about things like that. Besides, the child was only slightly injured and is doing fine."

That was the official party line and now, a hundred miles from the place that the incident took place, nothing was going to change it.

In spite of its friendly people, Uzbekistan was a police state. Eventually, Henning and Terry would receive back all of the belongings that had been stolen from them during their car repair, except for the $300 in cash. The official word was the villagers felt so bad for the theft that they had turned in the items to the police. The thought of what it really took for the army and the police to convince the villagers to return the gear makes me shudder. Leaving Uzbekistan was a pleasure.

Kyrgyzstan was one of the most beautiful countries of the entire journey.

The drive across Kazakhstan and into Kyrgyzstan was one of the most beautiful of the entire journey. I now understand why so many of the Soviet Union's mountaineers come from Kazakhstan. The terrain reminded me of Austria or Switzerland: high alpine valleys surrounded by snow-covered peaks. Sheep, goats and cows grazed alongside the highways and horse-mounted cowboys roamed the range trying to maintain some order. We toyed with some lyrics for a country-western song about being a Kyrgystani cowboy but couldn't quite make it work. The road surface was reasonable although occasionally there would be invisible ridges running across it which would shake the whole car. Surprisingly, gas stations were a common sight, and they even sold 95 octane leaded fuel. At one fuel stop we struggled to find a way to communicate with the four attendants in charge when suddenly one bright young girl, noticing that we were driving an old Mercedes-Benz said, "Ich spreche Deutsche!" at which point the rest of the transaction took place in German. A large number of German immigrants came to Kyrgyzstan after the First World War, and their grandchildren still occasionally speak German.

Another pleasant surprise was the town of Bishkek in Kyrgyzstan. It is modern, and even the old Soviet-era Pinara-Bishkek Hotel we stayed in had Internet access. We arrived in Bishkek on the 21st of May and we had been on the road virtually non-stop for three straight weeks. The strain was beginning to show on everyone, yet we were only a quarter of the way around the world. Each day we had faced new sights and experiences and by now we were feeling overwhelmed. There just wasn't enough time for our minds to process what we had seen before we were faced with a new day's adventures. But we had no choice but to press on. The next morning we had a special test on an airport runway inside the Bishkek city limits. Thousands of people arrived to watch us race, and the laughing and cheering crowd was in a good mood. Pretty girls wandered in groups from car to car to have their pictures taken, and the atmosphere was like a carnival. I spoke with one young woman who was a student and a reporter for the local newspaper and who understood English. She wanted to know all about our journey to this point and why we were driving through her out-of-the-way country. In fact, a surprising number of people in Bishkek were able to speak enough English to be able to ask about the cars or where we had come from.

Because the special test would only count for the teams that were finishing in Beijing, and would have no bearing on our standings, I decided that Mark should drive the course. It was frightening to sit in the passenger seat while he careened around corners and straights literally inches from the crowds that lined the course, and I suppose Mark looked at it as payback for all of the times I had scared him on those mountain passes. Thank-

A huge crowd gathered to greet us in Bishkek, Kyrgystan.

fully all of the cars made it through the walls of people without anyone being injured.

The drive from Bishkek to Nayrn in Kyrgyzstan through the foothills of the Tien Shan Mountains was beautiful. Crisp cool air and lush green valleys and a pass at over 9,000 feet invigorated the spirit. Along the way we saw many of the traditional yurts that the Mongols use for their homes. These large round tents dot the landscape, as they must have since the days of Genghis Kahn. Stopping on the roadside near a yurt was sure to bring several friendly people to the car, smiling and curious. Adding to the traditional appeal, the people in rural Kyrgyzstan still use horses as the most common means of transportation. Their beautiful animals are obviously a source of great family pride.

When we arrived at Nayrn our cars were directed to an old abandoned Soviet airbase and we were bussed some miles to a derelict former Army camp. Some chose to stay next to their cars and camp, guarded by several soldiers. This resulted in several reliable eyewitness accounts of what later became known as the Battle for Nayrn Airport.

There are two versions of this story. The one told by Philip Young on his web site describes a horde of marauding armed bandits that descended on horseback upon Nayrn airport in the middle of the night. Philip reported

The former Soviet Army base at Nayrn, Kyrgyzstan, was our jumping off point for China.

that these blood-thirsty terrorists were intent upon stealing our cars and equipment. The ever-vigilant soldiers guarding the cars managed to beat back the attack using their Kalashnikov machine guns. The pitched battle raged as the few competitors who elected to sleep near their cars cowered in fear.

I spoke with several of the cowering competitors afterward. They told a different story about what had happened. Six kids, one of whom was leading a pony, stopped to look at the cars. The competitors gave away a few pieces of candy and some pens while the kids practiced their English. They were cheerful and polite and interested in the cars. The guards were happy to accept some trinkets too. After a while, the road-weary competitors were ready for bed, but the kids wanted to stay. The guards tried to shoo them away, but they kept returning. Finally, one guard fired a shot into the air, and the children vanished. Such was the Battle for Nayrn Airport.

Meanwhile at the army camp in Naryn, sleeping arrangements were either in the remains of a barracks, or for a lucky few in traditional yurts. It was unclear how the choices were made as to who got into the yurts, an issue that would later be brought up by some of those who were obliged to sleep in the army barracks. Although the accommodations were crude, the views of snow capped peaks surrounding the town were magnificent. Food in the dining hall was plentiful, but sadly much of it was cold salads and eggs and some mysterious meat that few wanted to risk eating. By this stage, more than 40 percent of the competitors in the rally were already suffering from upset stomachs and the runs. We were all hungry, so Henning broke out a delectable can of meat that he had carried from his hometown of Braunschweig in Germany. With Swiss Army knives we spread it on pieces of bread we had taken from the dining hall. Sitting next to a babbling brook in the cold mountain air, munching on Braunschweiger on crusty bread was a fine way to spend our last night in beautiful Kyrgyzstan. There was some grumbling from the ranks about the inferior quality of the outhouses, but for the most part everyone treated it with good humor, realizing the next day would take us to that most forbidden of lands, China.

7

Forbidden China

China is an attractive piece of meat coveted by all ... but very tough, and for years no one has been able to bite into it.
— Zhou Enlai, Chinese Premier, 1973

The route we would follow into China was well traveled. In the second century BC, a Chinese adventurer named Zhang Oian made two incredible journeys from China into Central Asia that established what would become the Silk Road. Appointed as an envoy by the Han Dynasty Emperor Wudi in 139 BC, Oian was given the task of visiting the western Yue-chi tribes and convincing them to join the Chinese to help wipe out the Xiongnu who lived between them. While traveling he was unfortunately intercepted by the dreaded Xiongnu and held captive for ten years. His captivity can't have been too objectionable as during this time he married a Xiongnu woman and fathered a child. Upon his escape, he continued his diplomatic mission by traveling west along what would become the northern Silk Road, through the Taklamakan Desert to the town of Kashgar. The Yue-chi were not interested in a military alliance but assisted Zhang Oian in his further travels in the region.

Eventually, Zhang Oian headed back home. In an attempt to avoid the Xiongnu, he returned via the route that would become the southern Silk Road. He was captured once again, but this time managed to escape after just a year of captivity and without having fathered any more Xiongnu children. He finally returned to China after thirteen years on the road and reported on the geography and the existence of thirty-six separate kingdoms in the west that had been unknown to the Chinese.

By 100 BC the Silk Road was flourishing, transporting goods between China and Rome. The Romans had acquired a taste for Chinese silks and

121

spices, and the long journey was made in stages with the precious cargo traded from caravan to caravan until it reached the Roman Empire. The Chinese had extended their influence past the city of Kashgar, across the Tourugart Pass and as far west as Mary in Turkmenistan. Now the rally stood poised to enter China at the foot of that same Tourugart Pass in the foothills of the Tien Shan Mountain range.

The border between Kyrgyzstan and China lies in an all but deserted no-man's land at the center of the 10,000-foot Tourugart Pass. The organizers decided this would be an excellent opportunity to separate the competition field a bit by requiring an almost impossibly fast time for the rough 120 miles before the border. The road was gravel, with huge potholes, boulders and lots of washout damage. Tires, suspensions and frames all took a beating. At times the gravel was so thick that the car would sway sickeningly from side to side as it got caught in ruts. Other times the road would be washed out completely with a rugged detour to negotiate. We started out from Nayrn driving as fast as we dared over the deteriorating road surface and soon were passing cars that were moving slowly, either because the drivers did not want to damage their cars or because they already had.

A few of the heavily loaded rally cars broke their springs, several had structural failures of suspension mountings, and six cars had flat tires. The carnage was amazing. Ann and Peter Hunt broke a rear spring and had the front suspension collapse on their Austin Healey. They kept going at a slow pace.

Up until now, the rally had been a pleasant little jaunt compared to this brutal drive. Will and Carrie Balfour were hit by another rally car that misjudged the speed of their pre–War Talbot in the heavy dust. Our Mercedes kept pounding along, our stout skid plates absorbing most of the impacts and our Bridgestone light truck tires impervious to the sharp rocks. I tried to put out of my mind the thought of having to change to the two Michelin tires riding in our trunk in case of a flat and concentrated on trying to see through the swirling dust. It was frustrating to catch slower cars only to have them refuse to make room on the narrow roadway. With only one road to follow there was little navigation for Mark to do; instead, he acted as lookout for the worst potholes and boulders. I spent an eternity behind a late 1960's Rover, all but bumping them in their trunk in an effort to get them to let me pass. I was screaming obscenities at them as rocks occasionally bounced off the hood and windshield of our old Mercedes. Finally we found a slightly wider spot in the road, and I barged past them, showering them with rocks. They quickly fell behind us.

Nobody was catching us. It was hot and sticky in the car, and dust found its way through every seam. As we climbed higher into the pass the engine strained with the incline and the altitude. About fifteen miles before

Tourugart served as a rallying right of passage.

the finish the exhaust note of our engine abruptly changed, and we lost power. The exhaust pipe tip had been pounded closed by a large rock. Almost instinctively, I knew what the problem was, but we couldn't stop to fix it until the end of the section. Finally, after more than two hours of intense driving we arrived at the end, a mere ten minutes late on the section.

The exhaust problem had cost us a minute or two. A couple of the more powerful cars actually made the section on time as they were able to keep speed up on the long uphill grinds. One or two others dropped a couple of minutes. Most cars were at least 20 to 30 minutes late so we felt that we had done well with our old but tough Mercedes-Benz. At the finish, we stood next to our dusty and battered cars waiting for the Chinese border to open and feeling like we had accomplished something. To arrive at the western border to China having traveled over the Tourugart Pass was a rallying right of passage, and we were exhilarated. Every few minutes another car would arrive, and its occupants would be welcomed as heroes. By driving so hard on this section we passed more cars and had moved up to 19th place overall.

The Chinese border was divided into two parts. We crossed the first border station at the top of the pass and then entered a desolate uninhabited region for almost sixty miles. This would not be a good place to have a breakdown, and yet the roughness of the road resulted in even more damage to some overstrained suspension systems and ragged rally teams. Aside from the pinched exhaust pipe, our car felt fine as we crept along the bad road that occasionally detoured into a riverbed on our way to Kashgar in China. We now had plenty of time, so we didn't have to beat up the car too badly. The rugged section was especially unkind however to Barry Weir in his beautiful 1954 Aston Martin DB2/4. Weir (who went by his British title The Honorable Barry Weir in all of the official results and entry lists) was driving what had to be one of the least likely of vehicles for a drive around the world. The low slung Aston sports car suffered a complete suspension collapse and had to be loaded onto a flatbed truck. The process of loading also inflicted damage to the fragile bodywork of the stylish red car as it was transported to Kashgar. It wasn't pretty. Others limped through the rugged riverbeds, trying not to add to the damage they had already done to their cars getting over the Tourugart Pass.

We eventually emerged from the potholed gravel road and joined a major new highway that quickly opened into four lanes of blissfully smooth pavement. We made good progress and in a short time arrived at the official customs control into China. The place was jammed with Chinese officials, present to oversee the activity. The soldiers were all exceedingly formal, saluting sharply as we drove up. We could change money here at the border station, and Mark did so while I talked to the other rallyists and posed for pictures with the Chinese soldiers and police officers in the bright sunshine. In most of the countries we had visited so far U.S. dollars had been happily accepted, but in China we would only be allowed to use Chinese currency. The officials and police were polite but reserved although most wanted to have their picture taken next to one of the rally cars. After dozens of photographs and much shaking of hands and polite nodding of heads we were allowed to continue into China. We pushed north along a two-lane road for about an hour and entered the 3,000 year-old border town of Kashgar.

The Europeans rediscovered the Silk Road in the 1800s and gave it that name. A struggle for power between Britain and Russia in Central Asia in the nineteenth century had necessitated a route from west to east. In addition to spies and soldiers, reopening the Silk Road brought scholars and explorers who found the region to be filled with exquisite art treasures. They were duly shipped to museums in Europe, India and Japan. The most formidable obstacle in the Silk Road journey was the Taklamakan Desert. As we had learned from the briefing in London two years earlier, the name means "you may go in, but you will never come out." To bypass this inferno, the northern Silk Road skirted along the base of the Tien Shan Mountains at the top edge of the desert through the town of Korla and the Turfan

The imposing entrance to China. *Richard Newman*

Depression. The southern Silk Road went through the settlements of Yecheng and Hotan along the base of the Kunlun Shan Mountains north of Tibet before rejoining the northern section at Anxi. After having heard for so long so much about the fearsome desert, it was sobering to suddenly be here in Kashgar, on its western edge.

We had a day off in Kashgar, and it was a good thing. If we hadn't, a dozen or more cars wouldn't have been able to continue. Next to our hotel was a workshop, and its yard was littered with broken rally cars. Sparks from an arc welder flew and cars lined up for hours waiting for their turn for repairs. The sad rows of abused and broken classic rally cars reminded me of the scene from the movie *Gone with the Wind* of wounded soldiers lying on the ground in Atlanta.

Mark pulled the mangled exhaust system off of our car and found a Chinese mechanic with a sledge hammer who could open the pinched end. He also attached Chinese license plates to the front and rear of our car. Every car and service vehicle in the event was required to carry these special plates. We already had our Chinese Driver's licenses which had been applied for more than a year earlier. Nobody knew how strict the Chinese officials were going to be, and nobody wanted to take any chances this far from home.

Our hotel in Kashgar was in a great location. Before the First World

Repairs were an almost continuous prospect. *Richard Newman*

War the Kashkar Qinibak Friendship Building had served as the Russian consulate. The unused front lobby was elegant with beautiful chandeliers and intricate tile work. Only part of the hotel had been renovated, and this led to grumbling from competitors who were billeted in the unrestored section. It hadn't been the first time that some of the teams felt that others were getting special treatment when it came to accommodations. The unrest finally culminated in a general competitor's meeting to air these and other grievances that had been building for almost a month.

It is inevitable in such events that the main group splits into several sub-groups. A collection of many of the French and Swiss competitors seemed to gather around Claude Picasso for example. Mark had joined with a group of Americans whose primary interest seemed to be drinking as much beer as possible every night. I enjoyed hanging out with Peter and Ann Hunt from Scotland or Rich Newman, the Citroen driver from Chicago in my off time. One problem with group dynamics is that inevitably one group feels as though it is being shortchanged in the allocation of resources and information. The "they have it better than us" sentiment is a dangerous one, especially when it's true.

Everyone jammed into the hotel dining room as a belligerent Philip Young stood before the group with his team of organizers. The sense of "us against them" was palpable. The major complaint, charged primarily by a group of English and German competitors, was about the quality of the hotels in which we had stayed up until that point. This complaint had several of us scratching our heads. We hadn't seen too many four-star hotels along the route through the former Soviet Union. We stayed in whatever was available. Usually the only other hotels in town that might have been better were too small to accept all of the rally competitors and organizing staff. The most vocal group of complainers also felt that the organizers were taking the best rooms for themselves and leaving the dregs to the rest of us. These charges had been leveled against Philip's organization on previous rallies, probably by some of the same people who were making them now. His denials of this charge were quite vehement.

Several people also observed that some teams, notably the ones that whined and complained the most and the loudest (and coincidentally the ones most likely to come on future Philip Young events), were also finding themselves in the better accommodations. In many ways this made sense from a business point of view. By catering to repeat customers, Young was ensuring the long-term survival of his Classic Rally Association organization. With the Soviet army barracks of Nayrn fresh in our minds, it was an issue that made many angry. Only a small number of lucky teams had stayed in the nomad yurts, while the majority braved the crude army accommodations. Because it wasn't clear how the assignments were made, dissatisfaction resulted. The grumbling and complaining actually masked the major conflict: Some of the competitors had come for a tough adventure drive around the world and were happy with whatever came along while others had come expecting a pleasant stress-free vacation with five-star accommodations.

To me, sitting firmly in the camp of those looking for an adventure, the real problem was the psychology of some of my fellow travelers. When you are used to having the spotlight focused on and absorbed only by you, there is little light left to reflect onto others or onto the world that surrounds you. For the most part, the crowd assembled in this room were the economic and social elite of their home countries. They were not used to sharing the spotlight with anyone, and several treated the organizers as if they were the hired help. I also suspect for some it was also the first time that no amount of money or connections were going to change the fact that it was a hard, hot and dirty job to get the car from one end of the day to the other. Fortunately these people were in a minority. After all, we had come on this event to test ourselves in difficult conditions, and staying in third world accommodations whilst in the third world was part of the adventure.

The whining was getting pretty bad until Bill Secrest, the American who was driving the pre–War Chrysler Airflow with his daughter, Kelly, stood and spoke. Bill is a retired airline pilot and longtime rally competitor. With the same calm and reassuring voice that he would tell passengers that their flight was going to be cancelled, he reminded everyone that conditions were probably a lot worse when the New York to Paris around the world race took place in 1908 and that this was supposed to be an adventure. When Bill was finished, several of us noisily got up, served ourselves from the buffet and began eating as conspicuously as we possibly could. It was our own small protest against the childish behavior being exhibited by some of our fellow travelers. Not contributing to the whining seemed to take some of the hot air out of the sails of those who were complaining the loudest.

In 1908, complaints of favoritism had also been levied. The American Thomas team had been granted special permission to drive on railroad tracks across the American West to avoid some of the worst roads and washouts. The railroads refused such permission to the teams from other countries making their travel more difficult. The resulting bad feelings toward the Americans would last throughout the rest of the race.

Back in Kashgar, having diffused the impending revolution, important news about the event from Philip quickly followed. After years of preparation and months of route surveys, the original route along the southern Silk Road and straight across the legendary Taklamakan Desert would now

In 1908 the roads were rarely easy. *Courtesy of the Detroit Public Library, National Automotive History Collection*

be scrapped, and we would follow the northern Silk Road. This was a big disappointment as testing ourselves in the Taklamakan Desert was one of the big draws of the drive through China. Philip explained that the police had changed our route at the last minute and that the organizers had to scramble to work out how the competitive sections of the rally could now be run. The official reason for the re-route was that a recent sandstorm had covered the road across the Taklamakan and that it was now impassable. There was no possibility for discussion. The organizers told us that they only found out about this re-route upon their arrival in Kashgar, but later as we arrived at different cities along the new route, we were told by locals that they had known we were coming for several months. This was our introduction to how things worked in China. It also gave us a glimpse as to who was really running the show after we crossed the border into China. It was clear from the faces in the room that many were relieved that we would be spared the trial of the Taklamakan.

For once, little work was required on the car so I was able to catch up on my writing. When I was finished, I put all of my stories onto a diskette and walked across the street to John's American Café. No fooling, that was the name of the place. John himself was a tall Chinese guy who spoke reasonable English. In the back room of his café John had three computers that could connect to the Internet. I used one of them; and aside from having to use a slow server, I was able to send the stories and several photographs out to the waiting world. While I was there Kaya Busch came in to use the computer. Along with his brother, Sami, and father, Karl, he was running the event in a nearly stock mid-fifties four-cylinder Mercedes-Benz 190 sedan. They drove the car carefully and well, having few problems and were therefore highly placed in the overall standings. Although German by nationality, Kaya and Sami had both gone to college in the U.S. and spoke excellent English. Kaya was also regularly updating a web site and in a surreal way we frequently compared upload times and connection speeds from the most remote corners of the globe. I also called my contacts at National Public Radio (NPR) in Washington but nobody seemed to know anything about doing any follow-up interviews from China, and I eventually gave up.

Though we would not be traveling directly across the Taklamakan, our route on the northern Silk Road still meant we would traverse the top of the desert along the base of the snow-capped Tien Shan Mountain chain. For three days out of Kashgar we drove through the desert, first to Aksu, then Kuche and then to Korla. The drive was a bit like crossing west Texas, a lot of sand and some small scrub brush. The two-lane highway was often partially covered with blowing sand. The weather was hot and the landscape fairly bleak, except for the occasional small village where a cluster of trees would shade the mud-walled buildings.

Western China is a very much a frontier. *Richard Newman*

The towns of Aksu, Kuche and Korla were quite large and filled with incredibly curious Chinese. Just walking down the street in towns that seldom see western faces was enough to cause people to smile and small children to point and wave or sometimes giggle. Fashion in western Chinese towns is evidently a big thing, and short skirts in bright colors and platform sandals were all the rage among young women. Many were openly flirtatious with the western strangers.

The police were adept at keeping the large crowds away from the cars, but well-wishers still managed to get through to have their picture taken next to a car or shaking the hand of a driver. Some drivers of open touring cars complained about people sitting on their cars for such photos, but compared to the punishment we were inflicting on our cars during the day, it was hard to imagine how the soft derriere of a lovely Chinese woman could be catastrophic. The Chinese were not used to seeing classic cars and could be excused for not understanding the proper etiquette.

In Aksu, Mark and I had an interesting opportunity to discover how China is handling the information age. We had already discovered "Internet Cafes." These were places you could go to use computers and connect to the Internet for a small fee. Our hotel in Aksu was in the heart of town, and there were lots of shops and markets. We had been told that there might be an Internet site up the street so Mark and I walked that direction and started asking the shopkeepers for "Internet?" while wiggling our fingers as if typing on a keyboard. Most shook their heads, but eventually one pointed us to a large door in the back of a small alley. We knocked on the door, and a young man answered. I asked him if we could use the Internet. He looked at us briefly, nodded once, and motioned for us to enter. Inside the air conditioned room were perhaps a dozen computers each attended by four or five teenagers. Most were playing computer games with bright graphics splashed across the screen. Mark repeated the request, and the young man scribbled on a piece of paper and handed it to us. It said that he only understood written English, not what we were saying. The ultimate computer geek! I wrote that we would like to check e-mail on the Internet. He wrote back that it was almost time to close. Then he added that we should wait for a minute, and he picked up the phone and made a call.

After his phone conversation, the man wrote on the notepad that we should follow him. He carefully padlocked the teenagers in behind the big steel door, and for an instant I worried what would happen if a fire were to break out. They would be trapped. He didn't seem concerned. We followed our guide into a back alley and through three or four buildings. We went up staircases and down from building to building, until we finally reached the back of a building larger than the rest. We walked up six flights of back stairs and came to a door. The man knocked on the door, and it was opened. Inside was a small room with three computers and three men typing furiously. One of them was introduced to us, and our guide left us. Our only words in common were Internet and e-mail. It took some time, but Mark and I were both able to sign-on and retrieve our messages. I was also able to send out several stories and even a picture that I had brought with me saved onto a floppy diskette. After about 45 minutes we were finished and said goodbye to the three computer nerds tucked away in their hideout. They refused any payment and instead wanted our e-mail addresses to add to their lists.

As Mark and I left the building we exited from the front. I looked back and saw that we had been in the Chinese Telecommunication building, a part of the Chinese government. From this and our other online experiences in China, it is clear that while the Chinese government doesn't actually approve of the Internet, it understands that eventually it will need to have people who know how to use it. Everywhere we went, the electronic portals were hidden away, yet tolerated as a necessary evil. Since returning from China I have heard that most of the Internet Cafes have been closed down following a fire in 2001 that killed a dozen or more teenagers who had been locked in a small room, very similar to the one we visited.

In Korla, a car wash had been set up at the edge of the hotel parking lot. Most crews took advantage of this and had their cars washed by a crew of enterprising Chinese who had shown up just for that purpose. Overnight however, a huge sandstorm blew in from the desert, covering all of the cars with dust. Isn't that always the way? The next morning, the heavy haze of sand and dust filled the sky and created a murky light for the first part of our day's drive. The route from Korla to Turfan included crossing several low mountain ranges, following a path through deep canyons carved into sandstone. This was the eastern edge of the Taklamakan desert, and I felt a pang of sadness that we'd only skirted it, not challenged its full fury. The transition from the Taklamakan to Gobi deserts was apparent as we crossed over one of these ridges. Even though the word "gobi" means flat gravel desert, the sand here was immediately finer and more reddish in color. We were behind fellow Americans Pat and Mary Brooks in their old Buick station wagon through this section, and I was content to simply follow and enjoy the view. Pat is a lawyer in a small town in Iowa, and Mary does social work. They were the team that Larry Gustin from Buick had suggested that I contact when I had been looking for sponsorship. Gustin had come through for the Brookses, and their wagon carried the Buick corporate logos on its flanks. Following the bulbous old maroon Buick while coming through one particularly scenic gorge, through huge drifts of sand piled against towering cliffs, we suddenly broke through a gap between the rocks. There before us, stretching perhaps 100-miles wide was a valley with a spot of green in its center, the Turfan Depression. The effect was similar to looking eastward from the western rim across Death Valley, but the scale was much larger.

The Turfan depression is the second lowest spot on earth. Four hundred and fifty feet below sea level, it is remarkable not only for its lack of elevation but also because it was an important oasis on the northern Silk Road. More than a thousand years ago, the settlers in this area dug irrigation ditches to the mountains. Eventually these ditches were enclosed, and the sands of the desert covered them. The same tunnels from ancient times are still used to bring irrigation waters to Turfan. Melons, grapes and fruits of all types grow in this oasis. They even make wines from the grapes grown here.

Before reaching Turfan proper we had a 47-kilometer (29-mile) timed section that bypassed the new modern highway and included the original paved and bumpy road down into the Depression. This was our first real driving test since entering China. The temperature was hot, 100 degrees F or more, and the average speed required was quite high. Most cars managed to run this section without penalty, but some were late enough to add a few minutes to their score. We roared through several small villages before reaching the finish of the section at the outskirts of Turfan without penalty.

We would have the next day off, so upon our arrival Mark immediately made arrangements with a local body shop to have the dents from our accident in Greece repaired. Several other teams whose cars had body damage had already taken advantage of the talented Chinese auto body men, and now it was our turn. Our car went to the shop at 9 p.m. and was returned 8:30 the next morning. Although it would win no Concours awards, from five feet away it was impossible to tell that our fender had once been so horribly mangled. Even the paint color was a near perfect match. The charge for the overnight service was an amazingly cheap $175 U.S. in cash dollars, of course. Apparently the official government ban on U.S. currency could be bypassed when needed.

Although everyone needed a day off, it was brutal for teams needing to do the inevitable car repairs and maintenance. Temperatures soaring over a hundred degrees with a hot wind blowing in from the desert made any work outdoors thoroughly miserable. Lawyers, doctors and captains of industry were out in the hotel car park, sweating in the hot sun as they checked over their mechanical steeds. I sat for much of the day at my laptop computer, earning my keep on the event. Mark, on the other hand, hung out with some of the other Americans and drank Chinese beer. He had taken a course in Chinese on an audiocassette before leaving and had learned specifically how to order a cold beer. He had also learned the words for arc welder, figuring that was something that would come in handy. Mark was having trouble adjusting to the culture shock of China and admitted that he wasn't enjoying himself very much. I'm afraid I couldn't understand his attitude. To me, we had come all this way to be exactly where we were. The opportunity for a westerner to drive across China in a private car was a rare thing, and I was determined to savor every moment of it.

In the afternoon I signed onto a tour that had been arranged for the rally participants. In Turfan, the Chinese government is undertaking the excavation of a major ancient settlement at Jiaohe. Settled from the second century B.C. until it was destroyed during a rebellion in the 14th century A.D., Jiaohe was a major trading center. What remains today are foundations and walls of hundreds of mud adobe buildings, baked hard by centuries of desert heat. The city had a wide boulevard leading to government offices from the time when Jiaohe was the seat of the western region of the Tang Dynasty during the seventh century AD. After a walking tour of this interesting ruin, a subsequent bus tour of the local markets proved that the practice of selling overpriced trinkets to tourists is still part of Jiaohe culture, even after two thousand years.

For the next four days and almost 1,000 miles we drove across the seemingly endless Gobi Desert. Leaving the Turfan Depression, we had a short Special Test on soft sand through the desert before beginning a long section of rough road. The Special Test was short enough to seem point-

The ancient settlement of Jiaohe. *Richard Newman*

less, although a couple of cars managed to get stuck and had to be pulled free. The organizers were trying to maintain some aspects of competition to the rally despite the toned-down reroute mandated by the Chinese authorities. Everyone, rally teams and organizers alike, had fallen into a routine that involved checking out of the controls in the morning, driving all day across the unvarying terrain and checking into the finish control at the evening's hotel at night. Sometimes one hotel wouldn't be large enough to house all of the rally, and the teams that were sent to secondary hotels invariably complained the next day about their substandard accommodations and that others were getting preferential treatment. There seemed no rationale for who ended up where and Philip Young was almost never seen.

The Chinese are working hard to modernize their infrastructure, and road construction is a big part of it. Unfortunately, this meant that large sections of the original highways had been ripped up to make way for the new, and detours went on for many miles. In fact, over one 200-kilometer (124-mile) stretch we had everything from broken pavement to extreme washboard to fine sand to gravel to sharp rocks. More than a dozen cars suffered punctured tires in this section, but our light truck tires were performing without any problems. The dust in some sections was incredibly thick, and many teams opted to wear surgical masks to cut down inhalation of the swirling clouds. Our car seemed to leak dust into the passenger

Top: A lunch stop in Western China. *Bottom:* Roberto and Rita's Lancia enters a Chinese hotel compound. *Richard Newman*

compartment from every corner, and Mark and I were soon a uniform gray color from head to toe. It made no sense to put on clean clothes each morning as in no time they would be coated with the same coating of thick dust. Instead, we wore the same clothes day after day, and the odor in our car became ripe. The car did admirably although we did crack a rear shock absorber mounting which we later had welded in the hotel parking lot when we arrived at Hami in the Xinjiang Province. Others weren't so lucky, and every evening the harsh blue light from a welder lit up the parking lot as serious structural damage was stitched together in hopes that it would hold for another day.

The heat of the desert is exhausting in its own way, especially while driving on dust covered gravel roads. I was surprised to find that the window tinting from Llumar helped here as we could keep our windows rolled up without feeling too much of the heat from the desert or letting in additional sand and dust. I had doubted that the tinting would be of much value, but I was wrong. Mark had used the material on his Suburban on the Panama to Alaska drive, and he had been right in insisting that we apply it to our car's windows. Even with the tinted shield, by the end of the day it was easy to have consumed two or more liters of bottled water. Covered with dust and dirt and streaked with sweat, we certainly were a disgusting filthy sight as we pulled into a new hotel every evening.

If the diversions from the main route were bad, rally navigation in China was easy. At each major intersection, a police guard had been posted to ensure we stayed on the prescribed route. Thousands of men, women and children stood alongside the highway and cautiously waved as we motored past. Often they would take their cue from the police. If the police waved, so would the assembled crowds. If the police remained unmoved by our passing, the local crowd would be much more restrained. We waved at everyone. One section of roadway of more than 20 kilometers (12.4 miles) was posted entirely with women police officers. Stationed about a kilometer apart, most would smile and wave as we drove past.

Some roadways were completely closed to other traffic until the rally passed by. We were warned repeatedly that it was forbidden for us to make deviations from the route or even to make unnecessary stops along the way. The police were polite but serious, and it was clear there would be no negotiation on this point. On the other hand, when we stopped for the evening at our hotel, we were free to wander the streets and mix with the locals to our heart's content. Why we were less of a threat when out of our cars was unclear. Rich Newman was the Citroen driver from Chicago who had lent me his shower in Turkey. Rich and I would frequently take advantage of this open policy, and we went on many walks through the cities in the warm evenings. Rich had driven his same well-prepared yet tiny car from Lon-

Thousands of Chinese children lined the rally route. *Richard Newman*

don to Cape Town in one of John Brown's classic car rallies and had also competed in a similar model in Philip Young's Peking to Paris Rally in 1997. He also had traveled by motorcycle to some of the most remote parts of the planet, was a voracious reader and was by all estimates completely fearless. I enjoyed our evening constitutionals and hearing his views of the world of which he had seen so much. Sometimes members of other teams would join us on our forays into Chinese culture; but many, like Mark, were happier to stay in the hotel bar and unwind while chatting with others who also spoke English.

By now, after more than a month of rallying, Mark and I had worked our way into a daily routine. In the mornings, I would wake up first and take a shower. Usually I would pull on the same dirty clothes from the day before and pack my bag before heading out to the car and strapping it into place behind the driver's seat. I would then go in search of breakfast, usually finding Rich Newman or Americans Chick Kleptz and Bob O'Hara from the pink pre–War Marmon already at a table. Chick had made a fortune in the franchised restaurant business and had one of the world's most impressive collection of Marmon automobiles. Bob ran an auto restoration shop and was a talented driver and mechanic. The pair of them were early risers, and it was always a competition to see if I could beat them to breakfast. Not being a coffee drinker and in fear of gastric distress, I would have

Rich Newman repairs a tire on his Citroen 2cv. *Richard Newman Collection*

a cup of tea and eat some plain rice for breakfast. After this I would return to the car and check the oil and the tire pressures and give everything a once-over to reduce the chance of having problems on the road. Often I would find a package of cashews, a Slim Jim or a stick of beef jerky stuck under my windshield wiper, a gift from Chick and Bob in the Marmon. The entire back half of their big pink car was configured into storage bins and they had brought a huge assortment of American junk food with them to fortify themselves on the journey. I looked forward to these little food gifts on my windshield every morning. Working on the car was also a good time to catch up with other nearby competitors to find out the latest rumors.

Mark would bring his gear to the car about twenty minutes before our start time, and we would have a brief discussion to decide how we would approach the day before he went to breakfast.

As we were driving long days, it made sense for both of us to drive. I was designated to drive the tough competitive sections, and Mark drove many of the other sections so I could rest. Mark is a good sane driver, and I never once worried for my safety while he was driving. If possible, I liked to have Mark drive the first stretch each day. It gave me an excuse to stand around with the other navigators by the morning's start control and learn how everyone was doing.

A rally of any sort travels on rumors and this one was no different.

Although the organizers made an attempt to post official information every day, the real information traveled by word of mouth, and it was important to find out as much as you could. What's more, you could find out who was or wasn't getting along with their co-drivers and learn who was sleeping with whom. With a limited number of un-paired women on the event, the latter item was a matter of intense speculation at the morning time control.

We never stopped for lunch. Mark would eat a few of the high-energy food bars we had stored in the car and maybe two or three hard-boiled eggs he had taken with him from breakfast. From the start of the rally, most of the teams had become adept at stealing bread and cheese at breakfast so that they could make sandwiches for the day's midday meal. I would usually drink extra water and live with a grumbling stomach. I just couldn't face the awful energy bars Mark had procured or soggy improvised sandwiches. Besides, as we went deeper into China the breakfasts became less Western, and soon breakfast food that was suitable for lunch fixings was all but nonexistent. Stopping at Chinese roadside cafes and buying soda helped. I drank a lot of "Future Cola," whose advertising slogan "Future will be better" was either an oath of good wishes from the beverage maker or a promise for eventual improvement in the product. I never figured out which.

Some hotels were more elaborate than others.

At the end of the day before arriving at a hotel, we would make sure that we had fueled the car and that everything was ready for the next day. Anything that had broken during the day needed to be attended to right away as we knew there would be no time to fix it the next morning. It was a routine that was adopted by all of the other teams and was the only way you could ensure that your car would be in good enough shape to continue each day.

After the first week or so of the rally, Mark and I rarely had dinner together. There wasn't any animosity between us, just a difference in what we were looking for. He would usually find some of the Americans to eat and drink with at the hotel while I would frequently join up with Rich Newman or Peter and Ann Hunt from the Scottish Austin Healey team and venture out into the town to find dinner at a restaurant. Usually this engendered lots of finger pointing and laughter as we ordered as few waiters spoke English. Peter and Ann own a horse farm not far from Gleneagles in Scotland, and Ann works as a large-animal veterinarian. Ann is warm and caring and a good conversationalist while Peter, a former engineer from England, is a bit remote until you get to know him. I always looked forward to an evening meal with the couple. After dinner and following a walk around town and a packaged ice cream bar (the Chinese love ice cream and have vendors at almost every street corner) I would typically be in bed and asleep long before Mark returned to our room.

The race around the world of 1908 had followed a different route across Asia than our 2000 version was traversing. After driving across Japan, the cars were shipped across the Sea of Japan to Vladivostok. In addition to a shortage of gasoline, competitors had to contend with mud-covered roads as they pushed west across Siberia. Conditions were appalling as the road was in serious disrepair and had been made redundant following the completion of the Trans-Siberian Railroad some years earlier. Bridges collapsed, roads had to be rebuilt, and the cars were in constant need of repair. It took competitors more than two months to fight their way across the continent of Asia.

Our first sighting of the Great Wall came on the drive from Hami to Dunhuang. Admittedly it was just a remnant of the structure from the 2nd Century, still it was a reminder of a completely different China. As we covered ground from west to east I was struck with the same transitions that we had seen across the republics of former Soviet Union. In the western part of China the people are taller and showed much more Mongol influence. As we headed east, the people were becoming shorter in stature, with more of the facial features we typically associate with the Chinese. The architecture was also changing. Near the border with Kyrgyzstan, many of the dwellings in the countryside were low adobe mud with high walls

Tough going across Asia in 1908. *Courtesy of the Detroit Public Library, National Automotive History Collection*

surrounding them. Now, as we crossed the Gobi Desert the buildings were more typically block and brick construction.

In Dunhuang, The Silk Road Hotel was memorable. It was built by Chinese businessmen as a convention center and was both modern and western in its amenities. Surrounded by desert, it had beautiful wooden beams and huge hallways, and a quality that was in sharp contrast to some of the run down hotels we'd stayed in during our drive across China. Dunhuang was once an important staging post on the Silk Road. Just outside the town is the oldest Buddhist shrine in China — the Mogao caves. Some 500 caves are carved out of steep sandstone cliffs, and the earliest painting housed there dated from the fourth century ad. Ed and Beverly took a taxi to see the remarkable site while I worked on my car. If China ever decides to truly abandon its restrictions on tourism, this place will become a major destination.

Driving in China is fraught with peril. Traffic consists of pedestrians, bicycles (usually with three people on board), rickshaws, donkey carts, motorized tricycles, farm tractors, cars, small trucks, buses, and large trucks. At any point in time any one of the vehicles on the food chain may be trying to pass another. Two lane highways easily become three lanes during such passes and sometimes four vehicles end up sliding by one another. Trucks that break down (and this happens frequently) are left in the roadway, and a pile of rocks is placed a few yards ahead and behind the truck as a warning to other road users. When the truck is repaired or towed away, these piles of rocks are left behind as a souvenir of the breakdown, and are yet another hazard that the motorist must avoid. Road construction crews give little warning that they are at work, and half of the road might suddenly close just as you are preparing to pass a heavily overloaded truck or hay wagon.

Because of the change in route and the need for the organizers to improvise competitive sections for the rally, the whole field of cars would occasionally stop at a gas station in a small village. Huge crowds would immediately appear and the children would dash from car to car in search of trinkets. We had printed 400 post cards to hand out along the route, but they were long gone. At one stop, in a dusty parking lot a boy of eight or so came up to me while I was sitting out of the sun in the driver's seat of our car. The boy smiled and pointed to the row of pens that Mark had attached to the dashboard with some Velcro. I shook my head, smiled and held out my hand to show I didn't have anything to give him. Instead of running off however he stayed and peered closely at the interior of the car. I looked around and found a small bottle of watermelon-scented waterless hand-cleaner. I squirted some onto my hands, rubbed them together and then smelled them. I then held out the bottle and squirted a bit of the liquid onto his small hands. He rubbed them together, took a sniff and his face broke out into a radiant smile. Soon, there was a crowd of small children surrounding my car, each wanting to have his or her hands treated with the magic scent-maker. It made me smile to think I was disinfecting the hands of half of the children of that small town.

Soon, the children went off to search for the pens and pictures that the other teams were distributing. But the boy who had first visited me still stood nearby. I smiled at him again and searched around the car, finally finding a tin of Altoid® peppermints. I carefully opened the metal box, popped one into my mouth and sucked in my breath while making a funny face. I then took another of the "curiously strong mints" and placed it in the boy's watermelon-scented disinfected hand. He looked at it carefully before putting it in his mouth. Immediately his eyes got big, and he made the same sucking sound and face that I had. We both laughed. Again other children wishing to experience the Altoid sensation surrounded us. Soon a pretty young mother appeared to see what the children were up to. I handed her a mint and smiled. She nervously placed it one her tongue and then looked surprised. She began giggling, and I started laughing again. It was a fine way to spend a hot afternoon.

Driving to Lanzhou provided us with many other opportunities to see sections of the Great Wall. In places it was intact for hundreds of yards and in others consisted of a few piles of rocks. For a time we drove through beautiful fertile valleys and the weather was cool. Later the terrain changed and became more arid as we entered yet another desert. A huge thunderstorm with marble-sized hail met us as we drove through a mountain pass crossing the Qilian Shan range. As the hailstones hammered our windshield we could only pity those who were driving in open sports cars. We were leaving the Gobi and entering the Teneger Desert. The people were different here too. They were descendants of people who lived on the traditional Chinese side of the Great Wall.

From the time of our engine problem in Turkey I had been babying the car. Sure, we had driven fast over the Tourugart Pass where we had a chance to make up places on the competition. But in China it meant driving at a slow and steady pace throughout the day, putting as little stress on the engine as possible. It was brutally hot on our route across the desert, and I was worried that this might do damage to our head gasket. By driving slowly and putting little stress on the engine, I hoped to keep us in the rally. My caution frayed Mark's nerves, and he wanted me to drive faster, but I wouldn't. Because of the reroute and the need for the Chinese police to control every aspect of the event, we would invariably have plenty of time to make each of the day's controls. Others would go roaring past us and arrive early at the hotel and the blessed air conditioning. At our reduced pace, it would always take us an hour or two longer to make it to the control or to the hotel at the end of the day. It was frustrating, and Mark didn't share my opinion that the car needed such delicate treatment. I knew it was galling to be caught and passed by all of the perennial back markers of the event. But I knew we had used up our spare head gasket, and as long as it wasn't going to cost us penalty time, we were going to drive as slowly as possible and use up our own reserves of patience rather than the car. We remained in 19th place.

Pat and Mary Brooks in their 1949 Buick Woody station wagon were also taking it easy. The American couple had made it just four days into the Beijing to Paris Rally three years earlier before turning back because of mechanical problems. Now they were taking no chances, and Pat refused to drive quickly, even if it meant taking substantial penalties. Cautious and steady, in real life Pat is a lawyer in a small Iowa town, having grown up on a farm. With true Midwestern grit, Pat had taken the earlier failure as a personal affront and now he was doggedly determined to make it across China. He wouldn't let Mary drive, for fear that something dire would happen if he relinquished the wheel. Whenever Pat and Mary passed us in their Buick, I could almost hear Mark's teeth grinding together.

Lanzhou is an industrial city replete with oil refineries and chemical plants. The Lanzhou Legend Hotel, where we had a day off to work on the cars, was a modern western-style hotel with most of the usual hotel amenities. The car park was filled with people working on the damage caused by almost a week of constant pounding and abuse. Shock absorber problems headed the list, but axles and wheel bearings were a close second. Some of the cars were falling apart around their owners. The Laings in their 1952 Aston Martin Coupe were towed in almost every evening with yet another major structural failure. They were always remarkably pleasant and cheerful about it, but wound up spending each night across China at a different welding shop. A fifties Alvis convertible from England had its flywheel come apart, and a mechanic with a welder had tried to repair this too. Because spare parts are scarce and their cars are fairly simple, Chinese mechanics are adept at quickly repairing problems that would be terminal in more "civilized" parts of the western world. Welding appeared to be the most common way most things were fixed.

While Mark was otherwise occupied, I found a cardboard box and rounded up all of the power bars that were stashed in the various cubbyholes around the car. I was amazed that there were probably ten pounds of the vile things, and this after Mark had consumed probably a third of the ones we brought with us. I carried the box to the edge of the parking lot where a small crowd of Chinese people were watching the teams work on their cars. I handed a few of the bars out to the nearest spectators, and then left the box on the ground, next to the fence where they could be reached by the crowd. A few people politely took the bars, ripped open the wrapping and took a bite. Most of them then wrapped up the bars and threw them in the trash bin. Later, I walked past the box and found that it was still half-full of the power bars. I never told Mark where all of his power bars had gone.

Fortunately, aside from tightening a few bolts and checking our fluid levels, the only problem we found with our Mercedes was a leaking steering box that we had to fill with oil every few days. I also discovered our special Bilstein gas pressure rear shock absorbers that the engineers had told me were supposed to last the whole rally were leaking oil badly, and I replaced them with some of the spare Bilsteins that we were carrying. It was amazing how much abuse these old cars were taking and yet were still covering hundreds of miles the next day. Meanwhile, the Chinese guards allowed small groups of people into the car park to watch us work and to have their picture taken standing next to a car or shaking hands with a driver.

As we traveled across eastern Asia, it was clear that China is heavily involved in improving its infrastructure. And, that they are doing things

Parking lot security in China was tight. *Richard Newman*

in clever ways. Long distance phone service, for example, is largely based upon cellular technology rather than stringing hard wires over the vast distances involved. The Chinese are also heavily invested in road building, and new and smoothly paved highways are everywhere. Along these highways are huge new gasoline stations with twenty or thirty gas pumps. The stations are largely empty, as there are few private cars, but they are ready for the time when more people will be driving on the roads. China's auto industry is booming, with help from Volkswagen, Audi, Mercedes-Benz, General Motors, Toyota and just about anybody else who can get a foot in the door. At first it was thought by many car makers that the Chinese would want a specially-designed thrifty and practical "third-world" car, but it turns out that the Chinese don't think of themselves as being a part of the "third-world." What they do want is BMWs, Buicks, Mercedes-Benz and Audi models, just like the rest of the world, and they are getting ready for them. The brand-new gas stations we saw all had 95-octane gasoline, and the advice we had received from the organizers about modifying our engines to operate on 75-octane fuel turned out to be unnecessary. This was frustrating as lowering the compression had been expensive and had made our car sluggish, giving it poor performance on some of the speed tests.

The last three days of driving to Beijing were more interesting than the previous week had been. Instead of desert terrain, sections of green farmland along the Yellow River Valley were a welcome change. Although several speed sections were included in the route, the actual times required were easy to meet. Nevertheless, some teams still managed to get penalty points, and as they added up we hoped that they would eventually help move us up in the standings. For now, we were still stuck in 19th place.

Police presence was heavy, and at some points there would be a policeman or policewoman standing at every kilometer on the route. At intersections we would see long lines of traffic on the cross streets that were being held until the rally passed. It's easy to imagine how American or European commuters would react to being held up so that a procession of classic cars could amble past, yet people smiled and waved.

By now we were traveling in a much more densely populated part of China. The crowds in the towns we passed through numbered well into the thousands. In most cases they would politely wave and cheer from the edges of the roadway. The children from entire schools would stand in their brightly colored uniforms and cheer as we motored past. In some towns the crowds would press forward until there was less than a car width gap to press through as a sea of humanity engulfed us. It seemed insane as people pounded on the roof of our car and cheered as we sounded our air horns and siren. Mark was nervous about riding through such crowds and at one point began screaming obscenities at the crowd through the closed car windows. I really thought he had finally lost it. Then he pulled out a camera, and the crowds pressed even closer. It was bedlam as we tried to inch our way through the city streets with the police occasionally able to open a brief hole for us to lurch through. Whenever we cleared a town, Mark was noticeably more relaxed. He later admitted to me that he hated traveling in China, and the whole time we were there he couldn't wait to return to the U.S. Because we rarely talked about anything that wasn't directly related to car repair, I hadn't realized he was having such a big problem with it.

From Lanzhou we traveled to Yinchuan, the capital of the Ningxia Autonomous Region, a largely Muslim province. Once again, because of my American bias, I had assumed China would be fairly homogeneous in its genetic and social makeup; but nothing could be further from the truth. Traveling by car, it was clear to see that each geographic region was distinguished by people who had developed their own beliefs and societies. From Yinchuan we traveled through the characteristic semi-desert landscape of Inner Mongolia, crossing the Yellow River at Shizuishan and spending the night in the industrial city of Baotou. From there it was on to Zhangjiakou, a small town that had only recently been opened to foreigners.

On our final driving day in China, we were marshaled into a long single line of cars and set out from Zhangjiakou in a convoy to the Great Wall. The road we were traveling on was closed, and in deference to some of the

Top: Pat and Mary Brooks park their 1949 Buick Woody Wagon next to the Great Wall of China. *Pat Brooks. Bottom:* The road to Beijing.

early pre–War cars, speeds were held to 35 mph or less. Finally, after more than 3 hours we arrived at the part of the Great Wall that most Western tourists in China get to see. Hundreds of the rally competitor's family members and friends had been brought by bus from Beijing here to meet us, and both Mark and I had emotional reunions with our wives, whom we had not seen in more than six weeks. Later, at the modern Kunlan Hotel in downtown Beijing, I had a chance to step on a bathroom scale for the first time since leaving the U.S. I had lost 18 pounds on our drive across Europe and China. A diet of rice and steamed vegetables will do that for you.

Beijing is a modern city of more than 12 million people and is friendly to Western tourists. With just two days to see everything, the last thing Mark or I wanted to do was worry about the car. Yet the organizers had decreed that we would need to drive our car to the airport, and then wait around most of the day while they were checked into the freight terminal. It didn't seem fair and neither Mark nor I wanted to give up a day to do it. Our salvation came in the person of Mary Brooks, who offered to drive our car to the airport and take care of the shipping process. Pat might not let Mary drive his Buick, but we were more than happy to hand over to her the keys to our Mercedes-Benz. It was the only time Mary got to drive on the entire trip around the world.

The view of the rally from the Great Wall of China.

Tiananmen Square and the Forbidden Palace have become major tourist attractions and people living in Beijing speak rudimentary English, at least enough to practice capitalism with American visitors. The scale of the Square is staggering and everywhere we looked there were armed soldiers making sure that order was observed. Loree and I visited the Forbidden Palace, bought a kite shaped like a hawk in Tiananmen Square and ate at a backstreet restaurant. During the afternoon, we were approached by some younger people who spoke broken English and who said they were "art students." They led us to a second floor showroom on whose walls hung simple but beautiful traditional Chinese paintings. It was clear that this was a racket to sell the artwork, but it was nice and wasn't very expensive, so we bought a couple of pieces. Besides, it was fun to talk to the "students" and see some of Beijing behind the scenes.

For the London to Beijing runners, this marked the end of their rally, and the Japanese team of Kenji Ishida and Takatsu Aoki in a 1964 Datsun 410 won the Historic division of that rally while an English Bentley driven by Richard and Elizabeth Brown prevailed in the pre–War division. After 38 days and more than 7,400 miles (12,000 kilometers), we had attained an important goal. No matter what else happened, we had all driven across Europe and Asia. The cars that finished in Beijing would be loaded onto a ship for the long trip back to England. Our German friend, Henning Ulrich, would be leaving us with his diesel Mercedes-Benz, but his pickup navigator, Terry Maxon, was determined to find a way to continue on around the world. Our friends, Ed and Bev Suhrbier, loaded their battered Mercedes-Benz onto a ship bound for California. As they drove across China their engine suffered problems with its valve train and had to be jury-rigged together by the rally organizer's mechanics. Then, just two days from their finish, the latch failed, and the hood of their beautiful cream and red convertible folded itself over their windshield. They managed to beat it back down and tie it into place, but it wasn't pretty. Still, as they had started out by driving across America from Los Angeles to New York, they had now finished their own personal around the world driving adventure. The prize-giving party in Beijing was elegant and a bit sad as we bid farewell to the many friends we had made driving across Europe and Asia.

For the 38 remaining Around the World cars, we had only reached our halfway point. From here, a huge Antonov aircraft would fly the cars to Anchorage, Alaska, to begin the next leg of this fantastic journey. Fred Giles and his wife still held the lead in their 1968 Hillman Hunter, followed by the Porsche 356 of the Steinhauser brothers, the Brodericks in their Mercedes-Benz 250SL, the Peugeot of Yves and Arlette Morault and Roberto and Rita's slow and steady Lancia from Italy. Our U.S. Mercedes Team was no longer in contention for the overall honors, but we were slowly moving

Top: Short time for sightseeing in Beijing. *Bottom:* The Antonov awaits to take us to Alaska.

up and still very much a part of the event. We had finally moved up another spot and were lying in 18th position overall and had hopes that our speed in the rough sections and good reliability would move us up in the standings as our competitors continue to add to their penalties. From Alaska we would drive across the Canadian Yukon Territory and through British Columbia and Alberta before crossing the Northern United States on our way to another airlift from Newark to Marrakech. Then a quick dash across North Africa, Spain and France before we reach the finish line in London. At least, that was the plan.

8

North America

Be master of your petty annoyances and conserve your energies for the big, worthwhile things. It isn't the mountain ahead that wears you out — it's the grain of sand in your shoe.
— Robert Service

The Round the World in 80 days Motor Challenge was headed for Alaska. In the 1908 New York to Paris race around the world, after battling across North America in the wintertime and reaching San Francisco, George Schuster and his American Thomas teammates were instructed by the race organizers to take the first available ship to Alaska. The intent was to put in at Valdez and to then follow sled dog trails to the Bering Straits. In a move of incredible absurdity, the race committee supposed that competitors would be able to simply drive across the frozen straits from Alaska to Russia. Thankfully, the Thomas team never got far enough to be faced with this obstacle. As soon as they unloaded their automobile in Valdez everyone realized that an automobile was far too large to traverse the narrow dog trails. "Ours was the first car ever seen there, and the inhabitants welcomed us with a band and parade. But the snow was so deep that the Thomas could not be driven off the dock, and a sleigh ride of a few miles with Dan Kennedy, who operated the Valdez-Fairbanks mail stage, convinced Miller and me of the impossibility of driving through Alaska. Some drifts were higher than houses...," said George Schuster (*The Longest Auto Race,* 1966). The whole Alaska leg of the race was eventually cancelled. The Thomas team received new instructions to ship their car to Seattle and then on across the Pacific Ocean to Vladivostok in Russia. The Thomas automobile and its crew spent 26 days aboard two steamships and then drove across Japan before reaching Vladivostok. While this extra month was no doubt relaxing to the 1908 racers, an extra month of down time on a modern rally would be unacceptable, especially to the people with the money that allowed them to be there in the first place.

One of the keys to the success of today's long distance rallies has been the Russian-built Antonov cargo aircraft. As the Soviet Union fell apart in the early nineties, the Russian military became hard-pressed for cash. One solution was to rent out their pilots and aircraft in a wide variety of creative ways. For example, a well-heeled American can actually get a ride in a front-line supersonic Russian MIG military fighter if they are willing to pay enough hard currency for the experience. More common, however, has been leasing the lifting power of the mighty Antonov. This aging aircraft is still one of the largest cargo airplanes ever built. It can carry as many as 45 vehicles at one time over 3,000 miles, making it possible for an entire rally to cross an ocean in little more than a day.

After far too short a visit, my wife stayed an extra day to sightsee in Beijing with Ed and Beverly Suhrbier while the rally and I headed for Anchorage, Alaska. Our cars were carried on the Antonov, while the competitors were booked on a Korean Air flight from Beijing to Anchorage, via Seoul. Mark's wife, Donna, came with him to Alaska, and I was jealous of

There was a lot of excitement among competitors over the Alaska leg.

the extra time they got to spend together. The trip was uneventful, and upon our arrival we enjoyed the hospitality of Alaska automobile enthusiasts at Anchorage's Aviation Museum. I had been to Anchorage before. In the 1980s, I had participated in the Alcan 5000 Winter Rally, a 5,000-mile trek up the Alaska Highway from Seattle to Anchorage and back in the middle of winter. I had returned a few years later to run the summertime version of the same 5,000-mile rally. Mark had been here during the Panama-to-Alaska rally, driving his Suburban.

June is a great month to be in Alaska, and the long twilight of a far-northern evening made an outdoor cookout even more pleasant. It was fun to watch the float planes take off and land in the bay near the museum. Hamburgers, hotdogs and fresh salmon topped the menu. Most found it an agreeable change from the weeks of Chinese food of hit and miss quality.

The Antonov was late in arriving. In an eerie similarity to our crossing of the Caspian Sea, the Russian captain had decided to save fuel on the journey by waiting for the better lift afforded by cooler air in the evening. Several members of the organizing team were allowed to travel with the cars, including Philip Young, who later described the clattering and banging Antonov as "one-hundred million rivets all flying in close formation." It was past midnight before the teams were reunited with their cars.

We had the next day off to fix any residual damage from China and to service the cars. Unfortunately it was a Sunday, and it was hard to find any place that was open. The local Mercedes-Benz dealership invited all competitors driving the German cars to come to their shop to get serviced. They even had invited some of their more prominent local customers and set up a buffet of cheese and snacks. This seemed like a fine idea until each of the competitors was presented with a bill for the service, calculated at double overtime for having the mechanics work on a Sunday. Our bill for what effectively was an oil change and greasing the chassis was $400. After the exceptional treatment we had received from the Mercedes-Benz dealers in Greece and Turkey, this was a real slap in the face. Welcome to America. We had hoped to find a spare head gasket here, but they didn't have the one we had asked to be delivered to Anchorage. There wasn't much else we could do so we thankfully left the greedy clutches of the dealer and made arrangements to have tires mounted and balanced and an alignment done at the local Bridgestone dealer early the next morning before we started on the North American leg. I had arranged for the tires to be shipped to an Anchorage tire store several weeks earlier, allowing us to replace the two badly sized spares that we had picked up in Istanbul. It would also be a chance to put the car on a modern wheel alignment machine to put everything into shape after the brutal drive across Asia. Meanwhile, Mark was ecstatic to be back in the land of french fries and cheeseburgers.

The first day of driving in Alaska was an easy trip from Anchorage to Tok Junction. This was a beautiful drive along Glen Highway 1 which passes the Matanuska River and Glacier and the mountain ranges that define much of Alaska's appeal. Several teams saw moose, we saw a small red fox, and at least one team reported seeing a bear. We stopped for lunch in Glennallen at the Long Rifle Lodge with a view of the glaciers. An early arrival in Tok Junction gave everyone a chance to relax and to contemplate the next day's drive into Canada.

One of my favorite roads in the world is "The Top of the World Highway" between the tiny gold mining town of Chicken, Alaska, and famed Dawson City in the Canadian Yukon. It is a beautiful drive that runs for miles along ridgelines with spectacular scenery on both sides. The highway is pretty far from anywhere, so traffic is rarely a problem. It enters Dawson City via a ferryboat that crosses the fast-flowing Yukon River. Halfway along the road's length sits a tiny border post for the crossing from the U.S. into Canada. This border station isn't manned all of the time, and a sign at the border indicates that if the Canadian border guard isn't in, you should check in at the town of Whitehorse at your earliest convenience. Whitehorse is some 500 miles away.

Unfortunately for competitors the guard was in residence, time was tight on the section, and the border crossing was jammed with rally cars, growing ever later as the single border guard processed each car. To make matters tougher, it began to snow as we entered Canada. We were one of the first cars through this section and were surprised at how much snow had accumulated on the roadway. Not as surprised as Phillippa McLachlan and Christine Jones in a 1960 Rover sedan. They spun on the slippery stuff and ended up in a ditch. We arrived on the scene and quickly attached a towrope and pulled them back onto the road surface with our big Mercedes-Benz sedan. It was fun to be a hero and great to be on the other end of a towrope.

In our own way, we were repeating history. On the 1908 race, shortly after leaving Vladivostok, the German Protos team had gotten hopelessly bogged down in the mud. The American Thomas team came to their rescue. George Schuster described the scene: "We had gone perhaps twenty miles when we heard the noise of a motor going full throttle, and soon came up with the Protos. It was so deep in the mud that only the tops of the rear wheels showed above the mire. The three Germans and a Russian army officer guide were attempting to pry it out, but with the churning of the wheels it was sinking deeper.... Miller passed the Germans our towrope, and we pulled the Protos to solid ground. Lieutenant Koeppen uncorked a bottle of champagne and poured drinks by way of thanks for what he called 'a gallant, comradely act'" (*The Longest Auto Race*). The incident was pho-

Top: Heading out of Anchorage. *Bottom:* Into the Alaskan wilderness.

Top: The further north you go in Alaska, the more rugged the terrain. *Bottom:* Chicken Alaska on the Top of the World Highway.

tographed for *The New York Times,* and the famous motoring artist Peter Helck later did an oil painting of the scene. We forgot to take any pictures of our heroics, but I figured Phillippa and Christine at the very least owed us a bottle of champagne for our "gallant comradely act."

Dawson City hasn't changed much since the days of Jack London and Robert Service. It was always a bawdy frontier town although today in the summer months motorhome drivers vastly outnumber grizzled prospectors. The day after our arrival was technically another rest day, but the organizers had decided to add in a quick 100-mile timed section to run in the Bonanza Creek gold mining area outside of Dawson. The road was narrow and muddy as rain had fallen all of the previous night. In some spots it was quite treacherous, and heavy fog was present at higher elevations. We drove quickly but cautiously, mindful that the way for us to move up in the field was to both avoid any serious penalties and avoid breaking the car. As we drove higher into the mountains the fog grew heavier until it became difficult to find the correct route. A few teams took wrong turns, adding to their penalties, but we managed to find our way with just one wrong turn. The drive was good fun, splashing through mud puddles like a kid, with the car sliding sideways on many corners and plenty of big muddy holes to go blasting through.

From Dawson City we followed the remainder of the Top of the World Highway south to the Klondike Highway, heading toward the Provincial Capital of Whitehorse. In the middle of the day, however, we left the paved roads for a quick test section on a fast smooth gravel road near Carmack. The roads were smooth and fast, and the times were tight. This was finally turning into a real rally. It was becoming clear that the special test sections were going to all be on dirt roads and forest tracks and that the speeds were set much higher than they had been across Europe and Asia. The result was quite a shakeup among the top runners as several had mechanical problems. Others simply fell off the gravel roads in their attempt to stay on time. For us, the difficult driving was great fun and gave us an opportunity to move up against the opposition to number 17. Some competitors began grumbling loudly that they had expected the North American leg to be easier than the first half of the rally. Most Europeans hadn't imagined that there would be any dirt roads at all in the North America section of the rally. After all, aren't all roads in America paved with gold?

After a night's rest in Whitehorse, we continued south on the Alaska Highway before again leaving pavement for two tough test sections on gravel that totaled 136 miles. The dust was thick, and the road was tricky. Several cars went off on this section, including the highly placed Porsche 356 of the Steinhausers and our pals the Hunts in their Austin Healey. Both cars were pulled back onto the road and were able to continue. After the long test

Top: Dawson City, made famous by poet Robert Service. *Bottom:* Dawson's main street is evocative of the Gold Rush days.

Top: A muddy timed section in the Yukon. *Bottom:* An overnight stop on the Alaska Highway.

section we faced an additional 186 miles of dirt and gravel roads before reaching our nighttime stop in Watson Lake. The dust on the long deserted stretch was particularly bad and provided a strong incentive to drive fast enough to keep others from passing us. We hammered along, our Mercedes not missing a beat, and were among the first cars to finish that day.

For competitors, keeping the cars going was a continual chore but sometimes when they broke, the most unexpected events occurred. Tom Hayes from Ireland and Michael Greenwood from England broke the differential in their green 1955 Chevrolet. They went to the Chevrolet dealer in Whitehorse in the Yukon to look for a replacement. The dealer didn't have anything close to what they needed, pointing out that they *were* driving a 45-year old automobile. One of the mechanics in the shop overheard their conversation and said that he might have one at home. A half-hour later he reappeared with a brand-new 1955 Chevrolet differential, still in its original box. He had kept this part on a shelf at home for more than 15 years.

Even more remarkably, when the pre–War Lagonda M45 of Chris Claridge-Ware and Stephen Morley-Ham put a rod through the side of the engine block of the rare English roadster in the depths of the Canadian North, they figured their rally was finished. They contacted several North American Lagonda enthusiasts, and initially had no luck. They then received a fax that told them to sit tight. An Anchorage Lagonda collector, upon hearing of their plight, had the engine removed from one of his own two M45 sportscars, strapped it to a pallet and had it shipped by truck to the men so that they could continue. There can't be more than a handful of these cars in the world, and without this car collector's generosity, the team would have been stranded. His only stipulation was that they rebuild it before returning it to Alaska from England when they were finished with it.

The next morning, we drove from the Yukon Territory into British Columbia. The scenery changed from rolling hills to snow-capped mountains and fast flowing rivers in deep gorges. Our route followed the Cassier Highway, which had been gravel when I drove down it ten years ago

Mark pilots our Mercedes through Northwest Canada.

but was now predominantly paved. This was one of our longest travel days with almost 500 miles to cover and a special test on the Nass River Forest road. The test was expected to be quite rough, but recent logging meant the road had been graded and was smooth and fast. Unfortunately, our car developed a new problem: its transmission wouldn't stay in fourth gear unless I held the gear lever in place. It was an inconvenience, but not a serious problem. Our car was still running well, and we passed several cars while sliding through the loose gravel. When we arrived in the town of Terrace, British Columbia, I hurried the car to Kalum Tire Service to change the transmission mounts, hoping that they were causing our shifting problems. The mechanics at Kalum stayed late into the night working on wounded rally cars and helped me change the mounts, but our shifting problem remained.

The Thomas crew in 1908 had also suffered from transmission woes. Four miles inside of the Manchurian border, there was a loud cracking sound as six teeth broke off of their driving pinion, and oil began leaking from a six-inch crack in the transmission. Fortunately, the team had shipped spare parts ahead by rail, and five days later George Schuster had his Thomas back in the race. He also had the good sense to send a message to the Thomas factory in Buffalo to send another complete spare transmission and more spare parts ahead, routing the shipment by way of Europe.

The next day's drive to Smithers started out well for us when we saw a medium-sized black bear feeding by the side of the road, but our shift problem was compounded now by the reluctance of the car to shift into any of the gears. Our problems were minor compared to some others. Cautious Roberto and Rita's Lancia, still a front runner, had a serious crash, falling more than 60 feet into a ravine after the rear axle snapped. The couple were shaken; Rita went to the hospital for X-rays. They both were okay, but the car was badly damaged. Roberto was sure that in two or three days he could repair enough of the wreckage for them to rejoin the rally. There wasn't a straight panel on the little white Italian car and most doubted we would ever see the husband and wife team again. Later in the day, a 1940 Chevrolet Coupe had a gentle roll that damaged much of the sheet metal on the right side. Several other cars had minor off-road excursions with little or no damage.

In Smithers we took our Mercedes to the Ford Dealer and found the clutch linkage had come apart, the reason for the hard shifting. With the help of a mechanic, we put everything back together and tightened up the gearshift linkages, but a test drive showed the car still jumped out of fourth gear. That indicated some sort of internal gearbox problem, but we didn't have enough time to take the entire transmission apart before we needed to be on the road again. At least we could shift gears again while a bungy cord would have to suffice to hold the car in fourth gear.

From Smithers we continued across British Columbia to Prince George and Kamloops before arriving in Banff for another much needed rest day. Kamloops impressed me as a pretty place to live. Situated in a semi-arid part of the Canadian Rockies, it has beautiful views of mountains. The name comes from the Suswap Indian name "Tk'emlups," meaning where rivers meet. The area was first settled in 1812 by fur traders and became important both during the gold rush of the 1850's and when the Canadian Pacific railway came through in the 1880's. The city itself was incorporated in 1893 with a population of 500; it has grown to more than 77,000. From the second floor of our hotel, the car park filled with rally cars was impressively framed by the mountains.

As I came in from working on the car, I saw the rally leader, Fred Giles, surrounded by a group of locals. As I walked by, I heard him carefully explaining where we had been and where we were going and the intricacies of the event. Some time later, when all of the competitors had gone into the hotel for the evening, Fred was still standing in that parking lot with his group of local fans. He even had a color map of the world, with the route marked on it laminated to the hood of his car so that he could show peo-

Approaching the Canadian Rockies.

Igor Kolodotschko nears Banff in his 1940 Cadillac Coupe.

ple where we had been. I knew how tired I was feeling, and I suddenly appreciated the effort Fred was making on the event's behalf.

In Banff we had a day off. Our seemingly never-ending search for needed replacement front brake pads was solved when Heinz Bruns from HD Motors Ltd. in Calgary arrived with two sets of pads for our car. He'd read about our plight on our website and figured that he could help us out. He refused any payment for the parts and wished us luck on our journey. In the afternoon, we were told that there would be a car show for the local people down by the train station. Mark didn't want to go, but, perhaps inspired by Fred Giles' example, I found the place along with four or five of the other competitors. Few people turned out to see us. Later, I found a mall, got a haircut and found a pair of khaki pants to replace ones that were getting worn-out from weeks of travel. Mark did the laundry; it was that kind of day.

Before the event, most competitors figured the North American section would be quite easy. What they hadn't reckoned on was organizer John Bellefleur. John is a French-Canadian professional rallyist with decades of experience in off-road driving in Canada and the United States. He was aided by Ross Wood, another immensely experienced Canadian Pro-rally navigator. In fact, Ross had been the organizer of the Ontario Winter Rally that Mark and I had competed in with the borrowed Subaru, so we knew we suddenly had a pair of influential friends among the organizers. John and Ross had been told by Philip Young to make the North American section tough and to find as many dirt and gravel roads as they possibly could when they set up the route. They did their job well. Maybe too well.

The roads were as or more challenging than any we had been on before. Long speed test sections followed by even longer transit sections also on gravel roads. It was tough. Some competitors loudly complained that the roads were taking a toll on their cars and that teams had fallen off the roads during the speed sections while trying to stay on time. Two camps formed. Mark and I were in the minority that really enjoyed the tough conditions. We had come for a rally, and that was what Bellefleur and Ross were dishing up. Most competitors, on the other hand, wanted the organizers to do something to make life easier. They figured just driving around the world in an old car was hard enough, and the organizers didn't have to go out of their way to make it tougher. Ultimately, these forces that were lobbying for a kinder and gentler rally began to win out. Each day would we receive a set of reroute instructions (shades of China) that largely avoided the gravel roads on which we should have been traveling. Many of the special tests were shortened to be less abusive to teams and cars although many remained

Gravel roads were the norm at the beginning of the North American Section.

difficult to run in the length of time given. Our team's only chance to move up in the standings had been on the rough sections where other competitors were making mistakes, having problems, or just driving too slowly to be competitive. As we had been moving up steadily through the field, to say we were disappointed about the results of this new democracy is an understatement. The way I saw it, if people were so worried about damaging their cars because of the high speeds on the rough roads, they didn't have to drive them so fast. It was easy enough to not press the throttle pedal down quite as far. But everyone wanted to avoid penalties, and many were driving seriously over their heads and abilities.

Paradoxically, despite what they had been doing for the previous two months most of my fellow competitors were not really rallyists. In fact, most weren't even car enthusiasts. They were driving old cars because that was what the rules required. If it had required that they ride motorized tricycles, many of the same people would have still come on the trip. Originally, they had signed on for the adventure of making a trip around the world. Then, because most were successful business people with a higher than average amount of competitive instincts, it began to matter to them how they were placed. They didn't want to be beaten by another rich bloke in another old car. Now, because the event had turned into a real rally, thanks to the efforts of John Bellefleur, they whined because it was too tough. I didn't hide my position and remained a vocal dissenter in the call for a less demanding passage. I wanted to drive hard, do well and finish ahead of as many other cars as I could — especially ahead of those who were whining. The only way that was going to happen was with plenty of fast tough sections and so that was what I wanted.

In Banff, several cars that had been missing for several days rejoined the rally. Thomas and Maria Noor had decided that they didn't like driving on all of the gravel roads and took a brief vacation from the rally. They drove their 1966 Mercedes-Benz Cabriolet on a different route from Dawson to Banff with a stopover at a resort in Jasper. They took huge penalties for this diversion, but it didn't seem to upset them. Meanwhile, Rita and Roberto of the Lancia team rejoined the event after the accident that had been caused by a broken rear axle. Their car still looked battered and twisted, but it was back on the road, and they were still part of the rally. Roberto reported that during the repairs, the mechanics couldn't find one of the car's rear coil springs, so, they went back to the crash site with a shovel and found the spring, a spare wheel and a can of oil in the dense underbrush.

Leaving Banff we headed south. Several test sections were included in southern Alberta, and a light rain was mixed with snow as we crossed the foothills of the Canadian Rocky Mountains. This made driving more interesting, and it was hard to judge just how slippery the gravel and mud roads were becoming. We crossed the border into the United States at Chief Mountain, not far from St. Mary's, Montana, and spent the night in a seedy hotel alongside the railroad line in Shelby, Montana. It was not charming, and the noisy contingent of malcontents now had the accommodations in America to complain about. I had to side with them on that point. To make matters worse, we natives had bragged all the way across China how great the breakfasts in America would be. Mounds of flapjacks covered in syrup and butter, piles of bacon strips, hash browns, sausage and biscuits with gravy, were all promised when we crossed the border into the United States. Our first U.S. breakfast in Shelby consisted of dry cereal in little boxes and cold, stone-hard toast. It was terrible. So much for the American dream ... On the plus side, two rally friends from Duluth, Tim Winker and Randy Jokela, met up with the rally as it entered the U.S. and were now tagging along, taking photographs and writing reports for several magazines. It was good to see friendly faces.

Our first special test in the U.S. was a tough one in the form of a 52-mile section called Sixteenmile Road. It started out easy enough. Fast smooth dirt and gravel with high-speed corners. One of these corners, a blind right-hander four miles after the start, caught out poor Claude Picasso in his factory-built Mercedes-Benz 230SL. As he was rounding the bend with his car sliding nicely, he met an on-coming local car and tried to swerve to avoid it. Two wheels got caught in a ditch, and the Mercedes did a half-roll, sliding along on its side before finally regaining its wheels and coming to rest broadside across the road. When we passed the accident scene a few minutes later Claude and his navigator, Sylvie Vautier, were both out of the car and okay after their ride, but their car wasn't. The blue and silver Mercedes-Benz, reportedly built for the artist's son by the factory restoration shop in Stuttgart for an astronomical sum, was in bad shape. Its windshield was broken as was the glass on the driver's side. The left side of the car was heavily caved in, and the right front and right rear had suffered severe damage. We slowed, but Claude and Sylvie waved that they were all right, so we continued.

Next, the road tightened as it entered the hills. The surface began to deteriorate with large muddy ruts pulling at the wheels. We soon caught and passed the Steinhauser brothers from Luxembourg in their 1964 Porsche 356 Coupe. They were the same guys we had passed in the mountains of Greece when our car was so heavily damaged, and once again they were creeping along at a slow pace. The badly rutted road threw our old Mercedes from side to side, but the tough skid plates and underbody protection was absorbing the punishment. The road was amazing. Every corner was different and predicting whether the road would turn right or left or continue straight ahead over the numerous crests was impossible. On one corner, I entered at a good speed only to find a huge mud puddle in the road's center and a yawning cliff on the outside edge. The car slid sickeningly toward disaster, and only at the last instant did the front tires find some grip and turn us away from the drop.

"Nice job!" commented Mark, but I knew it had been just luck that we hadn't gone over the edge.

Three corners later at an evil right-hander with another cliff on the outside we discovered that not everyone was going to be so lucky.

As we approached the blind right hand bend, we recognized Stuart Onyett from one of the Austin Healey 3000s running up the road toward us. He motioned us to slow down and called out to us that all was okay and that we shouldn't stop. We carefully negotiated the corner at slow speed without seeing any cars or problems. After rounding the bend and looking back, however, I saw his red and white Austin Healey about twenty feet down the side of the embankment. What's more, further down the cliff, sitting upside down in a ravine was the white 1955 Jaguar XK140 Coupe of Do and Ans Meeus-Jonkers from Holland. We could see the team standing next to their Jaguar and reasoned that another rally car clogging the narrow road above the accident scene wouldn't be of any help, so we continued on.

The rest of the section got tighter and tighter, running between the steep rock walls of a canyon before opening back up and traversing several pastures, complete with cows that seemed to enjoy strolling on the road we were desperately trying to drive along. It was hard to shake the scene of the upside down white Jaguar, and I probably drove a bit more carefully than I had been driving. Finally, the section ended, and we hurried up the road to the hotel in Bozeman, Montana, to find out what had happened to our friends in the wrecked cars.

Rick and Stuart's Austin Healey slid off the road causing little damage. The rally support truck hooked a cable to them and soon had them back on the road. Likewise, Claude Picasso was able, with help, to patch his car together and drove it to the hotel in Bozeman where he and several other competitors worked through the night to hammer it back into shape. A Volkswagen Rabbit windshield was duct-taped into place and a pair of trailer taillights were used to provide rear lighting, allowing the Frenchman to continue the next day.

The Jaguar had sustained more serious damage. Its roof rack had taken much of the impact, and a stout roll bar and competition seatbelts had done their job. After the car ended upside down, Do and Ans had to cut their seatbelts with a sharp knife to get themselves out of the car. The elderly couple were a bit bruised and battered, and Ans received a lot of admira-

Off road disaster: a very slippery road caused a major off. *Bottom:* Although nobody was seriously injured, the crash looked scary. Both photographs from *Randy Jokela*

The Dutch Jaguar XK 140 Coupe was heavily damaged. *Randy Jokela. Bottom:* Claude Picasso's Mercedes SL looks significantly worse for its half roll. *Tim Winker*

Our own car proudly wears its coating of mud.

tion from her fellow rallyists when she refused to be given a ride to the hotel, and stayed with her husband and their car until it could be pulled from the ravine. The Jaguar's wheels were bent and the body twisted and it looked like a total loss. But the Dutch couple were convinced they would rejoin the rally and immediately set about finding a shop that could make repairs.

Frank Barrett of the *Mercedes Star* magazine was waiting for us in Bozeman. Frank had driven 700 miles from Denver to see the rally and bring us a transmission to replace the ailing one in our car. He had read about our transmission woes on our web site and had come to the rescue. We strapped the replacement gearbox into the trunk for a day when we would have time to change it and then set about investigating a new vibration that had begun in the driveline. After a short time we found the problem. One of the bolts holding the flexible rubber coupling together on the driveshaft had worked its way into the back metal surface of one of the mounting flanges. I remembered that the same bolt had been changed by an over-zealous mechanic in Kyrgyzstan, but I hadn't noticed that he had neglected to include a washer behind the bolt head. Now the bolt had loosened and was allowing the rub-

Repairing a bad wheel bearing on the way to Yellowstone. *Mark Rinkel*

ber coupling to move and vibrate. We were carrying a spare rubber coupling, but the bolt head was rounded off and we were unable to loosen it while lying under the car. We reasoned that it would hold through the easy day to Yellowstone Park and made plans to have a garage with a lift stay open late in Billings to help us change the coupling. Frank took us to dinner and was wide-eyed at the tales we told of our adventures to that point.

The next day Frank followed us south into Yellowstone Park. We needed to drive to Old Faithful, check in at a time control and then head north to Billings for our overnight stop. Mark was driving, and from time to time he noticed the car would pull abruptly to the right as though the right front brakes were grabbing. Suddenly, an awful grinding noise came from the front wheel, and Mark pulled to the side of the road. I jacked up the car and found I could move the right front wheel in and out almost two inches. The wheel bearing had failed, and there was nothing to do but change it with the spare parts we were carrying with us. It went smoothly, and after borrowing some extra grease from a passing Citroen we had the job finished in about an hour. We continued on, aware, however, that an ominous grinding noise from the driveshaft was getting worse.

We arrived at Old Faithful, had our control card stamped, and left minutes later. We decided to take the same route as we had driven into the park to shorten the distance to Billings. At first, all seemed well. The noise from our tortured driveshaft seemed no worse. Then, as we climbed a long hill we heard the rifle shot sound of a bolt flying out of the driveshaft coupling and hitting the transmission tunnel. A horrible grinding noise and the smell of burning rubber meant we were stuck. What's worse, our cell phone indicated that no service was available. Having chosen an alternate route to Billings there would be no friendly rally sweep truck with its team of mechanics to help us out. We were on our own. Mark hitched a ride to a telephone to call a tow truck while I sat next to the car and waited. From time to time, carloads of tourists would stop to look at the pretty creek I was stranded next to, but none of them came to inquire whether I was in trouble or needed help. I guess modern cars have become so reliable that nobody thinks that a stopped car may be in distress. From my view, waiting for Mark to return there wasn't much assistance they could offer.

Two hours later Mark reappeared with a tow truck. In a strange contract arrangement, tow trucks that operate inside Yellowstone Park are not

Our rally control was at Old Faithful.

allowed to tow vehicles beyond the park boundary. This meant that Derek Johnston could only carry us as far as Gardner, Montana, before releasing us to another towing service. In Gardner, we put the car on a lift hoping we could quickly change the flexible coupling and continue on our way. Upon disassembly however, we found that the aluminum piece that centers the driveshaft had also fractured. This was a part we hadn't thought to carry with us. We gathered up the pieces and set out on a long ride to Billings sitting in the cab of a rollback truck. Just as it had in Turkey, our stricken Mercedes-Benz once again needed a tow.

We were in low spirits when we arrived in Billings. Sure, we had made our check-in time with seven minutes to spare, but our car was immobile, and we were scheduled to leave at 7:27 the next morning. From the tow truck I had managed to call Tri-Star Pete, a Mercedes parts house in Arizona, on my cell phone and had arranged for a used replacement part to be sent to us, but it wouldn't arrive until mid-morning, and we were certain to miss our start time and receive big penalties. I went dejectedly to the hotel room to call my wife with the bad news. Just as I reached her on the phone, Mark came bursting into the room. The parking lot was filled with members of

Not again! A long haul to Billings, Montana.

various area car clubs, and he had found a person who knew someone who owned several old Mercedes models, including a few examples similar to our 220S Sedan. In a flash we were in a car heading 20 miles away to the town of Laurel. The teenager who met us at the door of a typical suburban home was named Henry. Henry's father collected old Mercedes-Benz automobiles and Henry himself drove a sharp dark blue 190 Mercedes from the late fifties, the smaller brother of our 200S model. Several Mercedes-Benz cars were in the driveway while others were in a storage building. Henry's parents weren't home, but he was sure he could help us with the parts we needed. We had brought our tools with us and asked Henry which car we could take apart. He shook his head, smiled and led us into one of the storage buildings where a stack of driveshafts awaited us. He pulled the part we needed off the nearest one and casually handed it to me. A half-hour later we were in the hotel parking lot replacing the broken driveshaft parts under the lights provided by the electric generator of a local Studebaker-owning old car enthusiast. Mark did most of the wrenching that night, as I had run out of gas from repairing the day's earlier mechanical maladies. As different as we were in almost every way, I was once again glad to have Mark as a teammate. It was past midnight when he finished the job, and we loaded everything back into the car. Ironically, just as we were leaving the next morning, an express delivery truck arrived with the parts from Arizona. At least we now had spares.

From Billings we headed east and then south, crossing into Wyoming for a quick test section at Devil's Tower. This was a muddy uphill battle on an extremely slippery road. Nobody could generate much speed on this section, and after the recent carnage most people were playing it safe and trying to avoid disaster. We arrived in Rapid City, South Dakota, happy to have finished the day in 15th place. Remarkably, Do and Ans Meeus-Jonkers and their battered Jaguar XK140 rejoined the rally in Rapid City. We had last seen them in Bozeman and figured that they were gone for good. A local Bozeman resident had been found who was restoring a similar Jaguar XK 140 coupe and had many of the parts that they needed. Working night and day at a British car restoration shop, they had put their rally car back together and were happy to be back among us.

In spite of the tight schedule the rally required, the organizers had made an effort to show the Europeans some of the interesting sites in North America. In addition to The Devil's Tower, the route passed the Crazy Horse Memorial, the Mount Rushmore National Memorial and The Badlands National park. The Badlands National Park was a real eye opener, with fantastic terrain unlike anything we had seen in any other parts of the world. Neither Mark nor I had ever seen it before; and, after the stressful previous days, it was nice to be a tourist. From there we faced a long drive to

Top: Approaching Devil's Tower in South Dakota. *Bottom:* U.S. Mercedes Team at the Badlands.

Jamestown, North Dakota, arriving just in time to see an immense thunderstorm roll across the prairie.

We were full of anticipation for our next day's drive, another long one from Jamestown to Duluth. We knew that in the middle of that day there would be a long special test section near Lake Itasca in Minnesota. We needed to do well on this section, both to put some distance on the Hunt's Austin Healey behind us and to gain on the Rover 80 Sedan, driven by Phillippa McLachlan and Christine Jones in front of us. The road was narrow and rough, the kind that I like to drive. It was a forest road that, while not closed, should have very little traffic. I started out driving as fast as I dared, running the car nearly flat-out and sliding through corners with abandon. At times the rear end would catch in the shallow ditches on the sides of the narrow trail, and the rear fenders would rub against the scenery. The surface had been graded recently. That is, half of it had been graded, and a large ridge of loose stones was left down the center. Hitting this ridge sent rocks flying and threw the car to the edge of the roadway. I tried hard and the car performed magnificently. We soon overtook the women in the Rover, then caught the Austin Healey of Rick Dyke-Price and Stuart Onyett. I had to stay behind them and their shower of rocks for a time but finally found a way past while climbing a blind hill. It was a dicey move, but I was driving as if possessed. Next, we caught the 1960 Rover Sedan of David Hughes and Tony Sinclair. I was banging every shift at maximum rpms, and the car was scrabbling for grip as I threw it into each corner and over every crest. About six miles from the end of the section we caught, and with some difficulty passed, the Steinhausers in their Porsche. They either didn't see us in our big white car, or didn't want to let us pass. I seemed forever destined to catch and be held up by the men from Luxembourg and their little Porsche coupe. I screamed across the finish line and brought the car to a stop with all four wheels locked and sliding on the gravel.

But something was wrong. A horrible knocking came from the engine compartment. I fearfully opened the hood, expecting to see a connecting rod sticking out from the side of the engine block. I was relieved to find that whatever the noise was, it was coming from the upper end. We didn't have time to investigate and had to continue on to Duluth or risk taking penalty minutes against the ones we had just won with such difficulty. Was it worth gaining against the competition if it meant damaging the car and jeopardizing our chances of making it back to London? I began to have flashbacks to Greece and Turkey.

When we got to Duluth the engine sounded terrible. What's more, the oil pressure, which until now had been rock steady, would dip whenever the engine idled. After clocking in at the final control of the day, I removed the valve cover and immediately discovered the problem. Both center cam support towers on the cylinder head had broken and were sliding uselessly back and forth. The cam was being held in place only by the front and rear supports. This was the same thing that had happened when we had incorrectly installed the timing chain in Turkey. But what had caused them to break? With no answer to this question, we began trying to find parts to repair our engine. Nothing could be found locally, and by 9 P.M. the best we could find were some parts on a used engine 200 miles away, south of Minneapolis. Suddenly I remembered we had the parts we needed in Michigan, on a used head in a machine shop in Ann Arbor, where the engine had been assembled. I called my pal, Peter Pleitner, in Ann Arbor and asked him to get the parts in the morning and put them on a Northwest flight that would arrive the next day. Early the next morning, after some chasing around to find the head which two weeks earlier had been sent to storage in a barn, Peter got the parts on a flight that arrived in Duluth in the late afternoon. This was cutting things tight as we only had one day to fix the car in Duluth.

Early the next morning I brought our ailing car to Foreign Affairs run by Mark Strohm and Jeff Hofslund. The shop had been suggested by local rallyist and writer Tim Winker. Here we planned to change the transmis-

Salvation in the form of Foreign Affairs in Duluth, Minnesota.

sion for the one we had been carrying since Bozeman, rebuild the starter, change our Bridgestone tires for four new ones, and replace the broken engine parts with the ones arriving later by air. Master mechanic Greg Peabody was assigned to our project and quickly removed the broken camshaft towers and starter and set to work replacing the transmission. Pat Price, a sometimes engineer on a luxury yacht and all around good guy, took our broken pieces to a nearby welding shop so we would have a backup solution in case the parts didn't arrive.

Once again, our misfortunes echoed those of the Thomas team on the 1908 race. Schuster had done the right thing by having a complete spare transmission sent further up the route by the Thomas factory. He would need it as in Russia his transmission failed again. It wasn't repairable and it took a delay of five-and-a-half days to travel by horse and buggy to retrieve the transmission. The unit weighed 600 pounds and took three horses to pull in a wagon. After another day spent installing the new transmission, the Thomas was back on the road.

Yves Morault was also at Foreign Affairs, and the Frenchman was in low spirits. The engine in his 1965 Peugeot had begun consuming water and probably had a blown head gasket. Another team of the shop's mechanics worked on Yves' car and changed the cylinder head gasket, but the problem remained. Finally, they decided that the cylinder head on his car was cracked. This could spell disaster for him and his wife, the co-driver. More out of desperation and pity than any sound mechanical practice, I lent Yves a can of our radiator sealant to try to reduce the problem. Surprisingly, this worked, and they were able to continue in the event.

Shortly after 5 P.M., Mark brought the package of parts from the airport. Peter had sent the entire camshaft with all four-support pieces, and we changed the whole setup to improve the odds against a repeat problem. By 7 P.M. all of the work was finished, but the clutch linkage chose that moment to come apart, and our now long-suffering mechanic, Greg Peabody, spent the next two hours sorting out this problem. Finally, close to midnight, our Mercedes rolled out of the shop under its own power. We had dodged yet another rally-ending problem, primarily because our car had once again broken just before a rest day when we could perform major repairs without penalty.

Because of heavy traffic caused by the Fourth of July weekend and dry dusty conditions, the next test sections were cancelled, and we drove them as a regular part of the route. This gave us no chance to move up in the standings, but since we had developed a new vibration from the driveline, we weren't too upset.

What was going on? Why was our carefully built rally car falling apart around us? Arriving in Marquette, I crawled under the car in a heavy rainstorm lying in deep puddles to see if I could determine what was causing the vibration. I checked the flexible joint and the driveshaft center bearing but couldn't find the problem. Finally, I gave up, hoping we would make the next day's long drive and find more time to sort out the problem. Exhaustion from weeks on the road were taking hold, and it was hard to do even fairly simple tasks without lapsing into a stupor. My wife's family, who live in Michigan's Upper Peninsula, had come to visit, but I was too tired and worried to socialize much.

The vibration got worse. As we drove toward Bay City, Michigan, on mostly dirt roads it became more and more serious. When we got to Bay City the car was almost undrivable. A crew of Ann Arbor friends had driven up to see the rally cars; and my wife, who was visiting Michigan from Virginia, brought our aging Golden Retriever, Harpo, to see me; but the tension over the drivesahft problem was heavy in the air. Mark volunteered to work with event mechanic Peter Banham, while I entertained my friends. If there was anyone who could figure out the problem, I knew it was Banham, who along with the other rally mechanics was performing mechanical miracles daily.

By this point, the novelty of driving around the world had worn off. It didn't seem all that special. After all, for the previous two months, everybody I saw each day was doing exactly the same thing. My life consisted of

Finding a vibration in Bay City, Michigan.

about a hundred competitors and organizers, and everyone in that circle was driving around the world. It was only when I saw the way my friends looked at the cars and the competitors that I realized anew that not everybody gets to drive around the world. They looked at us like we were from Mars. Looking over the battered and damaged cars in the parking lot I could understand their feeling that we must be insane, but also recognized the look of envy on some of their faces.

Halfway through dinner Mark came in and triumphantly reported that the rear bolts holding the driveshaft to the differential had come loose, and that had been the problem. The bolts were impossible to check without removing the rear skid plate which we had not done since before the start in London. Our drive the next day from Bay City to Niagara Falls, Canada, was blissfully free of vibrations. Mark's wife and children joined him in Niagara Falls, and we spent the Fourth of July on the Canadian side of the Falls watching the fireworks arcing across the river.

Chicagoan Rich Newman didn't enjoy his stay in Niagara Falls nearly as much. His tiny 2CV Citroen was entered in the pre–War category. (It was considered the continuation of a design that dated from the 1930s.)

Rich Newman's Fourth of July in Niagara Falls.

Because Citroen had built its 2CV model for decades, Rich took advantage of the rules that allowed updating and fitted his car with the disk brakes with which later cars were equipped. In the highly lax technical inspection at the start in London, Rich made no secret about his car's disk brakes, but now the organizers were demanding that he change them to the older drum type or face huge penalties. Perhaps this was because Rich's tiny economy car was in second place in the pre–War class, handily beating the expensive pre–War Bentleys. To change the brakes also meant changing to an earlier-style transmission, and Rich and his co-driver spent the day in a covered car park doing just that. Fortunately, because he had run the car in so many other events, he had both a huge stash of parts in Chicago and the experience in working on the car to do it quickly. It was one thing to have to spend all day fixing the car because something had broken, but it seemed very unfair to have to do the work simply because the organizers suddenly decided to enforce a rule that wasn't all that clear to start with.

We thought the trip from Niagara Falls to Newark would be straightforward and uneventful, but were again surprised. First, the route chosen, with an overnight stop in Binghamton, New York, was challenging and

Lunch at Brock Yate's Cannonball Pub in Wyoming, N.Y.

twisty. It covered more than a hundred miles in Pennsylvania and a significant number of dirt roads. Second, our timing chain tensioner failed shortly after leaving Niagara Falls, creating a horrible clattering as the timing chain rattled loosely inside the engine. At any moment, we expected our trip to come to an end with a broken chain. On the other hand, we were getting used to noisy clattering sounds, and this was just one more potentially devastating problem with which we had to live.

When we arrived at our overnight stop in Binghamton, New York, we were delighted to see Neil Dubey and a crew of mechanics from Star Motors in nearby Endicott. Star Motors had rebuilt the rear axle for our car before the event, and Neil and the gang stopped by at our hotel to see how we were doing and to check out the cars that were driving around the world. Upon learning about our problem, the guys from Star Motors went into overdrive, first calling to get a new timing chain tensioner sent to our hotel at the Newark Airport, and next trying to come up with a solution to help out during our drive the next day. They finally gutted a tensioner from another Mercedes-Benz model to rig up a part for our engine. At the same time they also found a brake drum to replace the cracked front unit on the 1940 Chevrolet and helped out two or three other teams with minor problems. These were good guys.

We had one more day of driving in North America. Rich Newman, stopping by the side of the road in upstate New York for a call of nature, was nearly arrested for indecent exposure. After the police state of Uzbekistan and the thousands of soldiers we'd seen in China, the very real threat to run him in by the state policeman seemed ludicrous. We had our own problems. Our jury-rigged timing chain tensioner failed almost immediately after we started in the morning, and Mark and I drove our car gingerly for the rest of the day on our way to Newark. We finally made it, and I was relieved to see a package containing our new parts at the hotel desk when we arrived. We would have one day off in Newark to repair the ravages caused by the North American leg of the journey. On our off day in Newark I was happy to see Dan Schmutte from TechSight, one of our sponsors and most loyal supporters. Dan had driven down from Pittsfield, Massachusetts, for the day to help me work on our car and get it ready for the final push through North Africa and across Europe. Several competitors gave Dan their shopping lists as he headed out to find an auto parts store in the Newark area. This kind of help can be invaluable when you are stuck with an immobile car in a hotel parking with no easy way to get to parts stores and service stations. While waiting for Dan to return from his errands, I gave an interview to a local television station and did a few small jobs on the car. The parking lot in Newark was, as it had been in places like Tashkent and Istanbul, filled with competitors who were working on their cars.

Later, after fitting a new timing chain tensioner, new shock absorbers, and new front brake pads, Dan and I went in search of a tire repair shop. Mark and most of the other rally competitors had taken a bus to Ray Carr's house for a party. Ray was in his eighties and was driving a pre–War Ford V–8 Cabriolet in the event. I really wanted to go to the party, but one of our spare wheels wouldn't hold air and I thought the problem was a punctured tire. We were surprised to learn at a nearby tire store that the steel wheel itself had a small crack near the welded reinforcements we had added before the trip. After a bit of searching we found DK Welding and Ron Burgess, the Vice President of Operations. Ron ground away the old weld metal and laid a beautiful TIG welded bead to stop the leak. It turns out that DK also did lots of defense contract work, and Dan Schmutte, a former Navy submariner whose TechSight division is part of General Dynamics, knew lots of the same people as Ron, who had done Navy contract work. After a quick tour around the immaculate welding and machine shop, Ron refused payment for his artful welding and sent us on our way wishing us luck in Africa. I regretted missing Ray's party, but at least I knew we were back in fighting trim.

Newark represented a milestone for me. Before shipping the car to London, I had driven our Mercedes-Benz here for the New York Auto Show. This meant I had now driven the 40-year old car completely around the world. True, we still had to fly to North Africa and run the rest of the rally, but no matter what else happened, I knew in my mind that I had made it around the world. Besides, with only two more weeks to go until we reached London, what else could go wrong?

9

Habit Forming

We are glad to have made the trip, but none of the three of us would undertake it again for anything in the world.
— George Schuster, 1908

The poor old thing really looked as if it had had a hard time. The white paintwork was white no more, for it was streaked with dirt of many, long miles. Bull dust was everywhere, inside and out, but it looked rather content and superior as it sat among its cleaner contemporaries.
— Innes Ireland, *Sideways to Sydney*

Psychologists tell us that if we repeat a behavior for thirty days it will become a habit. For more than twice as long, more than eighty slightly crazed individuals had been waking each morning, loading themselves into crumbling classic automobiles and spending the day negotiating the route devised by the organizers, dealing with mechanical maladies, and getting one day closer to the finish in London. Psychologically, the first forty or fifty days of the event had seemed relatively easy, but now we were in uncharted territory. No automotive rally in modern times had ever lasted this long. It was getting hard to stay focused on the tasks at hand even as the ultimate goal was coming into view.

Once again the huge Antonov was used to move the entire rally across an ocean. Competitors flew via Royal Air Maroc to Casablanca and then on to Marrakech, while the cars and organizers flew directly from Newark to Marrakech. After working on our car in Newark to prepare it for the rigors of Africa, we felt confident that the final 1,500 miles would be easy. Others were in more desperate shape. Two cars that were loaded onto the Antonov in Newark had to be pushed onto the aircraft. For several days at the end of the North American leg, the 1948 Fiat of Francesco Cirminna from Italy and Stelios Vartolomeos from Greece had been faltering. The

Top: Robert Moore works on the 1940 Cadillac in Marrakech. *Bottom:* The French 1942 Pontiac Chieftain looks the part in Morocco.

Top: Peter and Ann Hunt prepare their Austin Healey 3000 for the rigors of Africa. *Bottom:* Marrakech was just like it seemed in the movies.

engine in the tiny car was worn out. The solution was to have a new rebuilt engine shipped from Italy to Marrakech where it would be installed on the off day before the rally resumed its way across North Africa.

The other car that needed serious help was the 1929 Bentley Speed Six of German Helmut Karbe and American Don Sevart. On the final day in North America the timing gear inside the engine broke, leaving the car stranded. Karbe's solution was simple, but expensive. He had the big Bentley loaded onto the Antonov and flown to Marrakech with the rest of us, but instead of unloading his car, he then chartered the Antonov to carry his car back to England where his mechanics labored for three days to rebuild the engine. With a fresh engine, he headed south through France to rejoin the rally and finish with the rest of us in London. It put him into last place in the pre–War category, but he didn't care. He wanted to finish what he had started.

Marrakech was a bustling city full of exotic sights, sounds and smells. It was almost exactly what Hollywood would have you imagine North Africa is like, and a screenwriter could have scripted our visit to the downtown market, followed by lunch at a sidewalk café. The food was good, although later it left me feeling slightly queasy. After a pleasant interlude across North America we had returned to the lands of bottled water and dysentery.

On the first day out of Marrakech we faced the Tizi-n-Test, a twisty mountain climb that had been one of the most famous speed sections in the golden age of rallies in the 1960s. The road was narrow and steep, and in some spots the drop-offs over the edges had to be a thousand feet or more. Driving this tricky section was complicated by oncoming trucks that invariably were to be encountered while entering a blind hairpin with nothing but space where a normal road's shoulder would be. Guardrails were nonexistent. There is an old rally saying about drop-offs being so big that you might starve to death or that your clothes would be out of fashion before your car hit the bottom of the cliff. The drops were that big. I pushed fairly hard at first but noticed the temperature gauge beginning to rise and backed off to save the engine. The outside temperature was hovering around 115 degrees F.

Later in the day, we entered a region of the Sahara where cinematographer F.A. Young had filmed *Lawrence of Arabia*. Film companies continue to use it for movies that are set in the desert. We passed the Atlas Film Studio and hoped to see a few scantily clad Hollywood starlets, but instead, we saw sand. Lots of sand. Several cars were in real trouble from overheating during this drive. The worst was probably the 1934 Lagonda whose borrowed engine from Alaska would last less than 40 miles of desert driving before blowing out its coolant. Chris Claridge-Ware and Stephen Morley-Ham fought bravely with their beautiful overheating sports car for day after

Top: Morocco was well traveled. *Bottom:* Driving on ancient roads in North Africa.

day, typically making it into the evening's hotel hours later than everyone else. They were getting near the end of their rope.

After our aggressive push in the North American section we were sitting in 13th position with a chance to catch the all-woman Rover team from Australia and New Zealand in front of us. There was one final desert test section, and Mark and I were determined to drive it at the limit to try and make up the time. If we were successful, we would pass the women's team. The last competitive section would take place in the late afternoon, and we stopped at our hotel for lunch first. There wasn't much to do for several hours, and with the desert sun beating down the hotel's pool was most inviting. Like many of the others I took a dip but was concerned when I saw Mark having several beers with his lunch. On the other hand, I wasn't his keeper and besides I would be doing the driving on the upcoming tough section, and if he needed a drink or two to calm his nerves I figured it was his business. The test section was across open desert with detailed route instructions, a special map with the course drawn on it and large orange arrows placed in the sandmarking the course. We started off well, sliding the big Mercedes on the sand and flying over dunes. By the first of three

Morrocco was hot but fascinating.

passage controls we had passed three cars, including the women's Rover. So far so good.

Teamwork in a rally car is incredibly important and so is communication. The navigator reads the instructions and maps and then feeds information to the driver at exactly the right time so that it can be processed and the car set up for the next turn. When it works, it is a thing of beauty. A slight delay can really foul up the process. Mark had a habit of waiting until he could see the next turn before giving me the instruction. It worked okay if we weren't going too fast, but on the desert section we were flying. As we were approaching a sand dune at a high rate of speed, I sensed that the road would continue to the right after the hill and set the car up in a slight power slide to carry us over the dune. Mark, reading from the instructions said "over crest," and I smiled in satisfaction knowing just how the car would land in the middle of the right hand bend after the jump. Just as we left the ground, Mark read the rest of the instruction "then left…" I glanced to my left and saw the road had split with one track continuing to the right on the trajectory I was on while the route we wanted veered to the left. I swore, and as the car landed, flicked the tail around, got on the power and let the car slide off the road and into the desert, before regaining the correct road to the left.

"You might want to mention the instructions just a bit sooner," I said dryly.

Everything was going well. Mark was reading the maps to keep us on course, I was pushing hard to go as fast as I knew how and the car was performing beautifully. When we arrived at the next control, which we assumed to be the second passage control, we were horrified to learn, however, that we had short-cut the course and that this was the finish control. Somewhere in the sea of orange flags and desert tracks we made a wrong turn, missing the second and third passage controls, and taking a huge 30-minute penalty for each. The hour added to our score meant we wouldn't catch the Rover in front of us. In fact, the penalty meant that we slipped behind Peter and Ann Hunt's Austin Healey into 14th place. After a half minute of shouting at each other, I turned our car around and drove a half-mile back into the desert to help Yves and Arlette Morault, whom we had seen stuck in the sand in their Peugeot. It was our penance for such an unworthy performance. After pushing and pulling and finagling with a towrope, we finally had them free of their sand trap and we motored across the dunes to the huge tent that had been set up for a feast in the desert. I was still angry and upset and didn't feel like eating. I kept asking myself, "How could we have made such a stupid mistake?" But what I really wanted to know was after we had been through so much, how could Mark have let me down? He'd had the maps in front of him. He'd had the route instructions. I was disgusted. We drove in a convoy back to the hotel after dark.

From Morocco the rally headed north, across the Mediterranean Sea at Algerciras and from there passing Benidorm and Valencia on the way to Terrasa in Spain. The rally was winding down as we dashed across Spain and the Pyrenees and into France. These were leisurely days with plenty of time for lunch. In spite of the easier travel, I was morose over our mistake in the desert. Even though intellectually I knew we were a team effort, I

Top: Ships of the desert. *Bottom:* Rally cars in the Sahara.

blamed Mark for having misread the directions. If our car was notable for a lack of conversation before, it was now as quiet as a monastery. There just didn't seem to be anything to say. My brooding was a stupid way to spend the last several days of what had been a tremendous adventure, but there you are.

On the route from Clermont-Ferrand to Rouen in France, we had a pleasant lunch at a roadside bistro with David and Mary Laing, whose 1952 Aston Martin sports car had tormented them so in China. After hearing their stories of desperate all-night repairs and learning how often they had come to close to quitting, I began to gain some perspective about the minor screw-up in the desert. Always cheerful and optimistic, the British couple were my choice for the team that had overcome the most significant obstacles to keep going.

The pre–War Lagonda team was another that wouldn't give up, much to the admiration of all of the other competitors. Cooler weather away from the Sahara finally eased their overheating problems. Seeing how well these teams had handled greater adversity than an off-course excursion did a lot to make me realize how unimportant it was to worry about whether we

Heading across the Mediterranean.

were in 13th or 14th place. Besides, right about then our Mercedes gave me something else to think about.

Our starter which, had been repaired in Duluth, began acting up again, refusing to start the car after the engine had warmed. We also noticed the clutch would overheat and engage itself when we had to sit in long traffic lines. We didn't worry too much. We had come so far already, and London seemed so close.

Once again, there was an almost eerie similarity to the fortunes of the American Thomas team on the 1908 race. Just outside of Berlin and only a day or two from the finish in Paris, their clutch failed leaving the Thomas disabled on the side of the road. Disassembling and repairing the clutch took hours, and it was night before the tired old machine and its exhausted crew were back on the road.

On our last night on the road in France, I was standing by the entrance to the hotel when a large bus drove up. It contained Do and Ans Meeus-Jonkers' entire family. They had driven over from Holland as a surprise for the Jaguar team who had survived the bad roll-over accident in Montana. Children, grandchildren, uncles and cousins all converged on the Dutch couple. It was really quite moving. Do explained that he keeps the bus so that his family can go on trips around Europe together.

The P&O Ferry to Dover took us back to England, and the cars were marshaled at Brands Hatch racetrack about 40 miles from London. Although some friends and spectators were here, it was mostly just the competitors. It was an emotional scene as the drivers of this epic adventure congratulated each other, and we celebrated our achievement. We had all driven our old cars around the world. Crusty Ralph Jones, who had driven with his wife, Dorothy, in an immaculate Aston Martin offered me one of his trademark cigars. The English couple, well into their seventies, had driven their beautiful car carefully and had few problems. I accepted Ralph's cigar and lit up with a swell of pride. I was one of an eclectic band of adventurers who had driven around the world. We clocked in our final time control and were sent in groups of ten cars for the milk run to the finish line at Tower Bridge.

The finish for the American Thomas car in 1908 had been triumphant. George Schuster describes it: "Rolling at 50 miles an hour over a cobblestone road, we approached Paris. Nobody knew our schedule, but beginning at Meaux, 25 miles out, crowds began to cheer us. Bicyclists rode excitedly alongside. People tossed flowers to us. Summer evening diners in sidewalk cafes raised their glasses and shouted 'Vive la voiture americaine'" (George Schuster with Tom Mahoney, *The Longest Auto Race*, 1966). The Thomas actually arrived in Paris several days behind the German Protos, but because they had taken the time-consuming trip to Alaska, they were declared the winners of the race in 169 days. The third place Italian Zust team took another month and a half to finish the event. The Americans had won the first ever around the world race, and as Schuster said, "There was champagne and more champagne."

As I drove our car closer and closer to Tower Bridge, traffic became more snarled. Finally, moving to the entrance of the bridge itself, I breathed a sigh as I began to believe we would make it. Mark and I shook hands and agreed that we had finally done it.

Then traffic came to a complete stop. The bridge was opening to allow a boat to pass. I had to leave the car running, as I knew our starter wouldn't work. I also had to leave it in gear, as I knew the clutch would soon over-heat, and I wouldn't be able to engage first. Minute after minute passed by. The car began to creep forward as the clutch engaged, and I held it with the brake. Smoke started to fill the car. The clutch was burning under the strain. I had no choice but to switch off the engine.

As the bridge closed and traffic was ready to flow we were stuck. Our car wouldn't start, and we couldn't engage any gears. It was a nightmare come true. We were holding up traffic, and angry horns started blaring behind us. We had no choice. The van in front of us belonged to one of the organizers so we attached our towrope and were pulled the last twenty feet across the finish line. After covering 22,000 miles over 80 days, the pain was acute; but we were blocking the bridge and had to move the car. As we entered the car park of the Royal Mint, other competitors assured me that we had in fact finished the rally; but my heart was broken. To drive so far, and for it to end at the end of a towrope was almost more than I could bear. Later, when the car had cooled down and the traffic was lighter, Mark drove the Mercedes across the bridge and back to give it a chance to properly finish the rally. This time it did so under its own power and so deserves its finishing medal.

The scene at the finish at the Royal Mint was chaotic. The place was jammed with friends and family members who had come to welcome home the returning heroes. Buick had flown over several journalists from the U.S., and I saw some of my colleagues briefly. More importantly, my wife had flown to Europe to be there and she reassured me that we had in fact finished this marvelous madcap adventure. Later that evening we sat with Will and Carrie Balfour and several others who had driven pre–War cars in the event. To me, they were all heroes, working so hard to drive such ancient machines around the world.

The awards ceremony was disjointed with three separate rooms and video feeds to each. A fireworks display over the River Thames also seemed disconnected from the reality of the drive. The winner in the pre–War cat-egory was the Canadian team of Jim Walters and his cousin, Lennox

Top: Jim Walters and Lennox McNeely from Canada won the pre–War category in their 1938 Packard Touring sedan. *Bottom:* Yves and Arlette Morault from France struggled to the finish with their overheating 1965 Peugeot 404.

Top: Karl Busch and his sons Sami and Kaya did well with their 1956 Mercedes-Benz. *Bottom:* Pat and Mary Brooks drove carefully around the world in their 1949 Buick Woody Wagon.

McNeely, in a 1938 Packard. Second was the father-daughter team of Rich Newman and Julie Simon from Chicago in a Citroen 2CV (although Rich had driven with several co-drivers during the event) while another father and daughter pair, Bill and Kelly Secrest from the U.S. were third in the borrowed 1935 Chrysler Airflow. It was remarkable that three North American teams beat the Europeans so soundly at their own game.

In the classic category British teams dominated with Fred and Jan Giles in a 1968 Hillman Hunter winning overall. The Hillman was the same car that Linda Dodwell and Genny Obert had used to win the women's class in the Peking to Paris rally three years earlier. Throughout the event, Fred could be found out in the parking lot explaining to the crowds what route we would be taking and what it was like to drive on the adventure. From the start he had stressed that the first and foremost goal would be to finish, and he not only did that but won the event in the process. He and his wife made very good champions. Nigel and Paula Broderick in their 1967 Mercedes-Benz 250SL followed them home. Third were Edmund Holfeld and Justin McCarthy from Ireland in a 1965 Ford Mustang.

The three-man German team of Karl Busch and sons Sami and Kaya also had a nearly flawless run in their 1956 Mercedes-Benz 190 sedan. The 4-cylinder engine for this car was a brand new old stock engine from the shelves of the Mercedes-Benz classic center. Aside from a broken genera-

Mark and I finally made it to London. *Richard Newman*

tor bracket in Turkmenistan, it ran perfectly and was well-driven to fourth place overall and first in the Historic Saloon Car class. The Honorable Barry Weir and his navigator, Ron Brons, recovered from their 1954 Aston Martin's structural problems in China to finish fifth overall.

Yves and Arlette Morault kept pouring water into their 1965 Peugeot and made it to the finish in London in sixth place. Claude Picasso and Sylvie Vautier finished in seventh position overall, despite their crash in Montana. Their car, a 1964 Mercedes-Benz 230SL that was once as pristine as the factory could make it, looked like a refugee from a junk yard. Still, the engine was strong and powerful, and even with the damage, the car had made it around the world.

Jean and Paul Steinhauser, brothers from Luxembourg, also had few problems, driving their 1964 Porsche 356 to eighth place. Paul and Joanna Rolph from England had chosen a 1964 Mercedes-Benz 230SL for the adventure. During the drive across China, the air inlet hose between the air filter and the engine split, allowing huge amounts of dust to enter the engine. The dust wore the piston rings and cylinders so that the car began using large amounts of oil. The team also crashed into a farmer's fence during one of the fast sections on North America, but the inconveniences did not prevent them from finishing ninth overall.

Fred and Janet Giles were first overall in their pedestrian 1968 Hillman Hunter in the world's longest auto race. *Richard Newman*

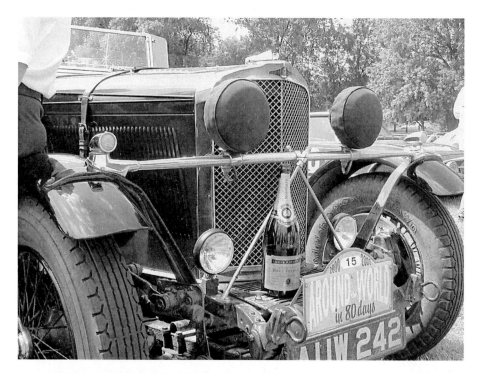

Top: Will and Carrie Balfour's 1933 Talbot deserves its Champagne. *Bottom:* It was a tough drive for some.

Our 1959 Mercedes-Benz 220S Sedan finished in 14th position and fourth in the Historic Saloon class. We were behind Rick Dyke Price and Stuart Onyett in their Austin Healey 3000; the two Rover sedans, one driven by David Hughes and Tony Sinclair and the other by Phillippa McLachlan and Christine Jones; and the Scottish Austin Healey of Peter and Ann Hunt. We had more problems than all of the other Mercedes-Benz teams combined, yet each time managed to limp the car along until we had time to do a proper repair. One of the great strengths of old Mercedes-Benz automobiles is their durability in the face of catastrophe.

Eighty days after leaving London's Tower Bridge on May 1st, 38 of the original 40 competitors who began the Around the World in 80 Days Motor Challenge made it back to Tower Bridge. Philip Young vowed that he would never again put on a rally around the world.

10

The Meaning of It All

"Veni, vidi, vici"
— Attributed to Julius Caesar

Not everybody gets to drive around the world. As Mark likes to point out, fewer people have driven around the world than have played professional basketball in the NBA. We did it the hardest way possible, piloting old cars on appalling roads and often driving through people's back yards. Most who went said they did it for the adventure. Adventure isn't always fun; and often it is hard; but it opens your eyes to the world and tests you in ways that ordinary life will not. Sometimes, no matter how hard you try or how ready you think you are, you do not succeed in the ways you had hoped to. Perhaps that makes you stronger. We covered more than 22,000-miles going around the world, with more than 18,000-miles of driving, and the part I will remember most vividly is the last twenty feet on Tower Bridge.

When I returned from London, I jumped into a move from Virginia to Ohio. My wife, Loree, finished her Hand Surgery fellowship at the University of Virginia and had accepted a job as a plastic surgeon at the Ohio State University. So a less than a week after my return to the real world, I was leading a cross-country caravan that consisted of four cars, two trailers and a dog. Thirty minutes into the drive, the radiator hose suddenly split on my Jeep. I jumped into my wife's car, went to a local auto parts store, bought the pieces to fix it and had us back on the road within an hour. A repair on the road of such minor magnitude didn't seem like a big deal, not after what I had been through. After all, this time my Jeep had broken down in a place where the people spoke English and where I could drink the water. How bad could it be? It sure as hell was better than being in Uzbekistan...

For some time after returning from the trip, I kept getting e-mail messages from the people I had been so close to during the past three months. It was as if they didn't want the adventure to end and were trying to prolong it by talking to one another. Many claimed that they had been profoundly changed by the whole experience, though when pressed they couldn't explain how. Others commented that after waking up each morning knowing exactly what they would be doing for the day ahead, they now had trouble figuring out what they should do with their lives. I kept waiting for a sense that I had been changed by the whole experience, but mostly, in the early days after returning, I felt the same as I had before.

Rich Newman, Pat Brooks and Mark had made an arrangement to have the three rally cars shipped back from London together in one shipping container. The cars arrived in Chicago in late September, and we decided that a party at Rich's warehouse was in order to celebrate our accomplishment. Loree and I went, and it was great to see everyone again. Mark and his wife, Donna, came and planned to drive the Mercedes from Chicago back to Cleveland where Mark would donate the car to the Crawford Museum. Loree and I stayed with Rich in downtown Chicago. Before Mark left with the car, I jumped in, pushed the starter button and was pleased when the old beast quickly sprang to life. Even the clutch seemed to be working. Sitting in the car felt natural, and in a way I envied Mark's opportunity to drive back to Ohio in the car that had taken the two of us so far.

Even before leaving London, everyone who had participated in the adventure was already talking about the next big event. Philip Young had announced that he would be running an event in 2002 from London to Katmandu. This seemed to have real potential, and I figured I could put together a team to do it. This time I wanted to do two things differently. First, as much as I enjoyed running the 1959 Mercedes-Benz sedan, I was taken with the idea of running a pre–War car. They have much more style, are simpler, and I wanted a bigger challenge. With contacts at Mercedes-Benz I knew that I could count on some help with such a project. I began scouting around and found that although most pre–War Mercedes-Benz models went for astronomical sums, the company did produce a four-door sedan called the 170V from the mid-thirties through the early fifties. It didn't take me long to find one, and I began the long process of getting it ready for the upcoming adventure.

The other thing I wanted to do differently had to do with my choice of co-drivers. Mark and I had gotten along as well as two strangers could have expected to. On more than one occasion his intelligence, stamina and resourcefulness had saved our collective asses. What I discovered driving around the world is that if you do an adventure of a lifetime, you should do it with someone whose lifetime you share. I decided that I wanted to make the run from London to Katmandu with my wife, Loree.

All of this changed on September 11, 2001. The route that Philip Young had proposed went straight across Afghanistan and Pakistan, and it was clear to everyone that the event wasn't likely to happen. Philip sent out notices that the event hadn't been cancelled and that his plans were going forward, but everyone knew that this was just wishful thinking. Finally, the Classic Rally Association quietly announced that the event was indefinitely postponed.

Even without Mr. Young's London to Katmandu adventure, my rally life was still proving busy. Pat Brooks had put together a deal to run the four-wheel drive division of the South American Inca Trail Rally in a brand-new factory-sponsored Buick Rendezvous. He asked me to go with him, and for two months we drove 15,000 miles around the perimeter of South America in the company of several of the teams that had driven around the world. Strangely, after two weeks on the road on that event, I realized that a year hadn't been enough time to recover, and I was already feeling the same kind of fatigue I had felt at the end of the Around the World jaunt. We eventually finished with a silver medal, but I hadn't found the event to be much fun. I followed this trip with a winter rally in my own 1967 Saab 96 rally car in Europe, enjoying the four days of driving with Marv Primack, one of my vintage racing pals from Chicago.

Mark and I used to joke that if our car had air conditioning, we would have qualified as Mercedes-Benz factory certified mechanics. After all, we'd had repaired every other system on the car at least once during our trip, and if we had A/C we would have probably fixed that, too. We had overcome all of the obstacles that stood in our way and had fought each day to get our car to the finish. In many ways it seemed like nothing compared to the perils that had faced George Schuster in the 1908 race, but that was then and this was now, and the world had changed a lot during the intervening 92 years. Besides, George had one day advance notice that he would be driving in the race around the world, and we had spent two-and-a-half years getting ready for our adventure.

Mark and I remain cordial, contact each other from time to time and are not really close friends. We are two very different people who shared an extraordinary time; it doesn't surprise me that we haven't remained closer after our adventure.

What had I learned from this trip of a lifetime? It is hard not to focus on the feeling of disappointment and devastation as we were towed across the finish line. To go so far, to do so much, and to come up short by a matter of a few yards remains painful. I joked with people that in thirty or forty years I would get over it, but the reality is that it hurt. It still does.

From the outside it's easy to be cynical about the whole endeavor. Who cares if a bunch of rich elitists drove their pretentious old cars around the world? We spent a lot of money and expended huge effort to do something that had never been done before and may never be done again. Was anyone saved? Creating a new sewer system or developing a new vaccine serves humanity, but it's hard to see how driving across the former Soviet Union or Communist China had much of a positive impact. The truth is driving old cars around the world is an impractical but terribly romantic thing to do. In 1908, the world was filled with romantic adventurers. There were poles to explore, mountains to climb, oceans to cross and worlds to conquer. The automobile and the airplane opened the doors to these adventures, and the men and women who were their masters were our heroes. When George Schuster and his crew drove the Thomas into Paris, they became international celebrities. The romance and hardship of their epic drive had captured the world's imagination.

There doesn't seem to be much room for romance today. Life, at least in the western world, is pretty easy by comparison to that at the turn of the last century. Cynicism and dissatisfaction have replaced wonder and enthusiasm. Joy has practically been outlawed. A malignant world view comes with the territory when you are an automotive journalist, but I had signed on to this adventure to have the same thrill that motoring pioneers like George Schuster had experienced. In the modern world, we often have to invent our challenges as Philip Young had done with the Around the World in 80 Days event, but does that make the challenge any less romantic? Cynicism kills romance, and perhaps that's why I was having such trouble coming to grips with how I had changed. I'd wanted the romance, the excitement and adventure, but those things are at odds with the process of daily living. I suspect that others on the trip were experiencing the same conundrum. Romance is a deeply personal thing, and I was trying too hard to rationalize the way in which driving around the world had changed me.

The meaning of our accomplishment crept in slowly, and if I was having trouble seeing the romance, others were not. To this day, people who hear of our adventures are wide-eyed with wonder and envy. More than a few have been encouraged to take on motoring challenges of their own, spurred on by the promise of adventure. Romance can beat cynicism given half a chance.

Meanwhile, over time I finally realized that aside from all of the romance and adventure mumbo-jumbo, the one real concrete lesson I had learned from having driven around the world was to never give up. When we crashed in Greece, we could have given up and gone home. We didn't.

When our head gasket blew and we almost wrecked the engine with an improper repair in Bolu, Turkey, we could have quit, but we didn't. The Saab team that shared our flatbed truck back to Istanbul gave up, but we didn't. In Canada when our transmission acted up, in Yellowstone when we lost our driveshaft, in upstate New York when the timing chain tensioner failed, it would have been easy to jump on an airplane and be home in a couple of hours. We didn't. We wanted to win. Maybe we could have won if everything had gone our way. It didn't. In fact many things didn't go our way at all, but we never gave up. I am proud of myself, I am proud of Mark, and I am proud of our battered old Mercedes-Benz. The sentiments may be outdated in our cynical age, but George Schuster hadn't given up and neither had we.

We had promised our sponsors and our friends, but more importantly we had promised ourselves that we were going to finish, and that was what we had done. Maybe not exactly in the way we would have wanted, but we had finished.

We also were able to see parts of the world not usually open to westerners. I expected China to be a drab and dismal place filled with people in Chairmen Mao jackets. I never expected to find it filled with color and life and excitement and with people who were friendly and curious and filled with good humor. I expected the former Soviet Union to be filled with criminals and prostitutes. Certainly we saw them, but we also saw more people who were just trying to get from one day to the next. American news coverage of the rest of the world tends to paint a picture that is almost completely the opposite of what you see when you travel by automobile to far-away places and exotic lands. I discovered that people really are pretty much the same everywhere. Aside from bothersome border crossings, differences in ideologies and governments mean nothing when you travel overland. What you find is that people who live in this world all basically want the same things. They want to have a home, they want to eat, they want to be safe and they want to have a life that brings them joy and maybe a little romance. The same is true for a teenage boy with his horse in Georgia, a woman in her yurt in Kyrgyzstan, a Chinese farmer driving a rolling haystack across the Gobi desert, or an Alaskan millionaire who just sent the engine from his pre–War Lagonda to help out a pair of Brits who needed it. Everywhere we visited, people went out of their way to help us, to entertain us and to try to understand us.

As I said in the beginning of this book, there are some things that are better after having done them than they are while they are being done. Would I do it all again, if I had a chance? Absolutely. I would go in an even older car, and I would go with someone I cared about. I would try to spend less time competing and more time visiting the places along the world. That would be hard, because I have finally accepted the fact that I am a competitive person who hates to lose.

In our age when telecommunications and the Internet are bringing people closer together, I realize now that maybe the most important discovery I made during this grand adventure is this: Anyone who says it's a small world hasn't tried to drive around it.

Appendix 1: Rally Route and Schedule

May–July 2000

Date	From	To	Distance (mi.)
London to Istanbul			
May 1	London, England	Chantilly, France	263
May 2	Chantilly, France	Aix les Bains, France	371
May 3	Aix les Bains, France	Santa Margherita, Italy	307
May 4	Santa Margherita, Italy	Ancona, Italy	338
May 5	Ingoumenitsa, Greece	Thessaloniki, Greece	304
May 6	Rest day in Thessaloniki, Greece		
May 7	Thessaloniki, Greece	Istanbul, Turkey	366
May 8	Rest day in Istanbul, Turkey		
Istanbul to Beijing			
May 9	Istanbul, Turkey	Bolu, Turkey	198
May 10	Bolu, Turkey	Samsun, Turkey	295
May 11	Samsun, Turkey	Trabzon, Turkey	248
May 12	Trabzon. Turkey	Batumi, Georgia	109
May 13	Batumi, Georgia	Tiblisi, Georgia	248
May 14	Rest day in Tiblisi, Georgia		
May 15	Tiblisi, Georgia	Baku, Azerbaijan	100
May 16	Turkmenbashi, Turkmenistan	Ashkabad, Turkmenistan	357
May 17	Rest Day in Ashkabad, Turkmenistan		
May 18	Ashkabad, Turkmenistan	Chardzhou, Turkmenistan	403

May 19	Chardzhou, Turkmenistan	Samarkand, Uzbekistan	248
May 20	Rest day in Samarkand, Uzbekistan		
May 21	Samarkand, Uzbekistan	Tashkent, Uzbekistan	248
May 22	Tashkent, Uzbekistan	Bishkek, Kyrgyzstan	372
May 23	Bishkek, Kyrgyzstan	Nayrn, Kyrgyzstan	211
May 24	Nayrn, Kyrgyzstan	Kashkar, China	223
May 25	Rest day in Kashkar, China		
May 26	Kashkar, China	Aksu, China	200
May 27	Aksu, China	Kuche, China	158
May 28	Kuche, China	Korla, China	162
May 29	Korla, China	Turfan, China	226
May 30	Rest day in Turfan, China		
May 31	Turfan, China	Hami, China	257
June 1	Hami, China	Dunhuang, China	260
June 2	Dunhuang, China	Zhangye, China	403
June 3	Zhangye, China	Lanzhou, China	321
June 4	Rest day in Lanzhou, China		
June 5	Lanzhou, China	Yinchuan, China	298
June 6	Yinchuan, China	Baotou, China	335
June 7	Baotou, China	Zhangjiakou, China	304
June 8	Zhangjiakou, China	Beijing, China	143
June 9	Rest day in Beijing		
June 10	Rest day in Beijing		

Anchorage to Newark

June 10	Arrive in Anchorage, Alaska		
June 11	Rest day in Anchorage, Alaska		
June 12	Anchorage, Alaska	Tok, Alaska	322
June 13	Tok, Alaska	Dawson City, Yukon	187
June 14	Rest day in Dawson City, Yukon		
June 15	Dawson City, Yukon	Whitehorse, Yukon	376
June 16	Whitehorse, Yukon	Watson Lake, Yukon	456
June 17	Watson Lake, Yukon	Terrace, British Columbia	535
June 18	Terrace, BC	Smithers, BC	293
June 19	Rest day in Smithers, British Columbia		
June 20	Smithers, BC	Prince George, BC	329
June 21	Prince George, BC	Kamloops, BC	410
June 22	Kamloops, BC	Banff, Alberta	342
June 23	Rest day in Banff, Alberta		
June 24	Banff, Alberta	Shelby, Montana	398

June 25	Shelby, Montana	Bozeman, Montana	304
June 26	Bozeman, Montana	Billings, Montana	340
June 27	Billings, Montana	Rapid City, South Dakota	488
June 28	Rapid City, South Dakota	Jamestown, North Dakota	487
June 29	Jamestown, North Dakota	Duluth, Minnesota	535
June 30	Rest day in Duluth, Minnesota		
July 1	Duluth, Minnesota	Marquette, Michigan	448
July 2	Marquette, Michigan	Bay City, Michigan	448
July 3	Bay City, Michigan	Niagara Falls, Ontario	345
July 4	Rest day in Niagara Falls, Ontario		
July 5	Niagara Falls, Ontario	Binghamton, New York	332
July 6	Binghamton, New York	Newark, New Jersey	207
July 7	Rest day in Newark, New Jersey		

Marrakech to London

July 8	Travel day from Newark, New Jersey to Marrakech, Morocco		
July 9	Arrive in Marrakech, Morocco		
July 10	Rest day in Marrakech, Morocco		
July 11	Marrakech, Morocco	Ouarzazate, Morocco	257
July 12	Ouarzazate, Morocco	Erfoud, Morocco	248
July 13	Erfoud, Morocco	Tangier, Morocco	409
July 14	Tangier, Morocco	Murcia, Spain	329
July 15	Murcia, Spain	Terrasa, Spain	369
July 16	Terrasa, Spain	Clermont-Ferrand, France	387
July 17	Clermont-Ferrand, France	Rouen, France	329
July 18	Rouen, France	London, England	183

Appendix 2: Rally Results

The following is a key to the countries in this appendix.

Symbol	Country
AE	Arab Emirates
AR	Argentina
AU	Australia
AUT	Austria
CDN	Canada
CH	Switzerland
D	Germany
DK	Denmark
F	France
GB	Great Britain
HK	Hong Kong

Symbol	Country
I	Italy
IRL	Ireland
J	Japan
LU	Luxemburg
NL	Netherlands
NZ	New Zealand
PL	Poland
SE	Sweden
USA	United States
ZA	South Africa

London to Istanbul Rally Finish

Position	Car#	Driver/Co-driver	Vehicle
Pre-War			
1	33	Stephen Harman (GB) Steven Harman Jr. (GB)	*1952 MG TD
2	9	Jens Pilo (DK) Anne Pilo (DK)	1933 Rolls Royce Phantom II

*Vehicle allowed in race because it was based on a pre-war model.

Classics and Historics

1	98	Adrian Pope (GB) Julian Reddyhough (GB)	1966 Aston martin DB6
2	62	Michael Joseph (GB) Ron Strasser (GB)	1961 Bentley Continental S2
3	82	Michael Weidernauer (AT) Johann Winterleitner (AT)	1963 Mercedes-Benz 220S
4	100	Andrew Powell (GB) Elkim Pianim (GB)	1964 Facel Vega 6
5	51	Irvine Laidlaw (GB) Marshall Bailey (GB)	1957 AC Ace Bristol
6	45	Jan Pearce (GB) John Heffer (GB)	1955 Triumph TR2
7	73	Conor McGauley (IRL) Darren Walker (GB)	1964 Mercedes-Benz 220SE
8	70	Henry Kozlowski (GB) Melody Revelle (GB)	1968 Austin Mini Cooper
9	46	David Spurling (GB) Patricia Spurling (GB)	1953 Morgan +4
10	86	Ralf Quistorf (D) Hans Wachsmith (D)	1967 Mercedes-Benz 250SE
11	96	Michael McRobert (GB) Lola McRobert (GB)	1972 Bentley T-series
12	57	Robert Filmore (GB) John Filmore (NL)	1955 Jaguar XK140
13	49	Icky Kurgan (ZA) Avril Kurgan (ZA)	1957 Bentley S1
14	102	Hanswerner Wirth (D) Dr. Ursula Schmitt (D)	1959 Jaguar MK IX
15	94	Gavin Sheppard (GB) Valerie Meachan (GB)	1968 Lotus Elan S4
16	61	Robert Perkins (GB) Brian Gadd (GB)	1966 Rolls Royce Park Ward
Retired	66	Frank Gump (U.S.A) Stephen Whitman (U.S.A)	1959 Mercedes-Benz 220SE

London to Beijing Rally Finish

Position	Car#	Driver/Co-driver	Vehicle
Pre-War			
1	29	Richard Brown (GB) Elizabeth Brown (GB)	1939 Bentley 41/4 MX Park Ward
2	11	Mark de Ferranti (GB) Sandra Ziani de Ferranti (GB)	1936 Rolls Royce Phantom III
3	5	Charles Kleptz (U.S.A) Robert O'Hara (U.S.A)	1928 Marmon Model 78 Sedan
4	10	Johannes Walenhamp (NL) Foppe D'Hane (NL)	1925 Bentley Speed Model
5	36	Klaus Von Deylen (D) Chris Von Deylen (D)	1952 Daimler DB18 Consort
6	7	Peter Noble (GB) Sue Noble (GB)	1925 Lanchester 40hp Tourer
7	4	Richard Wills (GB)/ Mark Wisniewski (GB) / Henry Cator (GB)	1914 Rolls Royce Silver Ghost
Retired	8	Don Saunders (U.S.A) Roger Coote (GB)	1932 Packard 903 Convertible
Blown Engine	1	Richard Seeley (GB) Gerald Michelmore (GB)	1912 Locomobile Type 48
Classics and Historics			
1	69	Kenji Ishida (J) Takatsugu Aoki (J)	1965 Datsun 410
2	65	Jean-Paul Lhotellier (F) Marie-Francoise Lhotellier (F)	1962 Peugeot 404
3	71	David Jones (GB) Myfanwy Jones (CDN)	1961 Jaguar 150S
4	26	Abdul Aziz El Accad (AE)/ Mariam El Accad (D)/ Jonathon Prior (GB)	1968 Rover P5
5	56	Anders Wulf (SE) Ingeer Wulf (SE)	1964 Volvo PV544S

6	55	Tom Harris (GB) Valerie Harris (GB)	1955 Jaguar XK140 Coupe
7	47	Chris Denham (GB) Ron Bendell (GB)	1954 Alvis Grey lady
8	72	John Moodie (GB) Thomas'Mathew (GB)	1964 Mercedes-Benz 220SE
9	92	Marc Treves (CH) Denis Langer (CH)	1965 MGB GT
10	43	Victor Thomas (GB) Hugh Marriage (GB)	1958 Morris Minor
11	97	Andreas Hobi (CH) Jurg Sturzenegge (CH)	1966 Ford Mustang
12	35	Henning Ulrich (D) Klemens Suchocki (PL)	1960 Mercedes-Benz 190D
13	19	Alastair Inglis (GB) Robert Inglis (GB)	1954 Peugeot Commercial
14	60	David Moffatt (GB) Bruce Thomason (USA)	1961 Bentley S2 Saloon
15	48	Edwin Suhrbier (USA) Beverly Suhrbier (USA)	1959 Mercedes-Benz 220SE Cabriolet
16	39	Gerard Besson (F) Marie-Odile Besson (F)	1957 Renault Frigate
17	64	Bernard Legrand (CH) Jean-Philippe Salzmann (CH)	1965 Mercedes-Benz 190
18	95	Peter Hopwood (GB) Ian Rhodes (GB)	1968 Jaguar S-Type
19	101	Patrick Brennan (GB)/ Inigo Edsberg (GB)/ Tara Lee (GB)	1959 Mercedes-Benz 190SL
20	44	Hans Reinhardt (CH) Annick Reinhardt-Quellien (CH)	1949 Willys Overland
21	25	Pierre-Henri Mahul (F) Jacques Mahul (F)	1967 Morgan +4
22	59	Daniel Spadini (CH) Eric Moullet (CH)	1959 Jaguar Mk 1
23	93	Charles Holt (GB)/ Adam Williams (GB)/ Peter Batey (GB)	1968 International Scout

Retired	74	Ricardo Fox (AR) Silvia Calderwood (AR)	1965 Mercedes-Benz 220SE
Off Road	87	David Stonely (GB) Dennis Pomfret (GB)	1964 Austin Healey 3000

Around the World Rally Finish

Position	Car#	Driver/Co-driver	Vehicle
Pre-War			
1	23	James Walters (CDN) Lennox McNeely (CDN)	1938 Packard Touring Sedan
2	18	Richard Newman (USA) Julie Simon (USA)	*1952 Citroen 2CV
3	20	Kelly Secrest (USA) Bill Secrest (USA)	1935 Chrysler Airflow
4	27	Janet Chisholm (GB) David Robinson (GB)	1940 Chevrolet Coupe
5	34	Francois Chervaz (CH) Shirin Azari (CH)	*1953 Citroen 11B Traction
6	15	William Balfour (GB) Caroline Balfour (GB)	1933 Talbot AV105 Alpine
7	28	Richard Ingham (GB) Judy Ingham (GB)	1939 Bentley MX Park Ward
8	12	Chris Dunkley (GB) Jan Dunkley (GB)	1935 Bentley Tourer
9	32	Igor Kolodotschko (GB) David Ellison (GB)	1940 Cadillac Coupe
10	17	Francesco Ciriminna (I) Michele Ingoglia (I)	*1948 Fiat Millecento
11	14	Chris Claridge-Ware (GB) Stephen Morley-Ham (GB)	1934 Lagonda M45
12	22	Raymond Carr (USA) David Dabbs (GB)	1939 Ford V8 Convertible
13	16	Helmut Karbe (D) Donald Sevart (USA)	1929 Bentley Speed Six
Retired	2	Bill Borchert Larson (USA) Terry Maxon (USA)	1913 Rolls Royce Silver Ghost

*Vehicle allowed in race because it was based on a pre-war model.

Classics and Historics

1	89	Fred Giles (GB) Janet Giles (GB)	1968 Hillman Hunter
2	91	Nigel Broderick (GB) Paula Broderick (GB)	1967 Mercedes-Benz 250SL
3	99	Edmund Holfeld (IRL) Justin McCarthy (IRL)	1965 Ford Mustang
4	42	Karl Busch (D)/ Sami Busch (D) Kaya Busch (D)	1956 Mercedes-Benz 190
5	54	The Hon. Barry Weir (GB) Ronald Brons (NL)	1954 Aston Martin DB2/4
6	63	Yves Morault (F) Arlette Morault (F)	1965 Peugeot 404 Coupe
7	90	Claude Picasso (F) Sylvie Vautier (F)	1964 Mercedes-Benz 230SL
8	84	Jean Steinhauser (LU) Paul Steinhauser (LU)	1964 Porsche 356 Coupe
9	88	Paul Rolph (GB) Joanna Rolph (GB)	1964 Mercedes-Benz 230SL
10	58	David Hughes (HK) Tony Sinclair (GB)	1960 Rover 80 Saloon
11	79	Rick Dyke-Price (GB) Stuart Onyett (GB)	1959 Austin Healey 3000
12	50	Phillippa McLachlan (AU) Christine Jones (NZ)	1960 Rover 80 saloon
13	83	Peter Hunt (GB) Ann Hunt (GB)	1962 Austin Healey 3000
14	76	Kevin Clemens (USA) Mark Rinkel (USA)	1959 Mercedes-Benz 220S
15	77	Ralph Jones (GB) Dorothy Jones (GB)	1961 Aston Martin DB4
16	37	Paul Bassade (F)/ Michel Magnin (F) Dominique Byramjee (F)	1942 Pontiac Convertible
17	81	Han le Noble (NL) Joop van Kesteren (NL)	1964 Porsche 356 Coupe
18	41	Tom Hayes (IRL) Michael Greenwood (GB)	1955 Chevrolet Sedan

19	38	Xavier Beaumartin (F) Phillipe Rochat (F)	1953 Studebaker Commander
20	52	David Laing (GB) Mary Laing (GB)	1952 Aston Martin DB2
21	31	Pat Brooks (USA) Mary Brooks (USA)	1949 Buick Woody Wagon
22	53	Dominicus Meeus (NL) Johanna Meeus- Jonker (NL)	1955 Jaguar XK140 Coupe
23	75	Roberto Chiodi (I) Maria Degli Espoti Chiodi (I)	1964 Lancia Flavia Coupe
24	78	Thomas Noor (D) Maria Bouvier-Noor (F)	1966 Mercedes-Benz 250 SE Cabriolet
25	85	Peter Hall (GB) Adrian Nash (GB)	1964 Facel Vega 6
Retired	67	Richard Taylor (USA) Dave Pierce (USA)	1968 Saab 96

Appendix 3: U.S. Mercedes Team Sponsors

Mercedes-Benz North America — entry fee, shipment of car and new parts
Bridgestone Firestone — entry fee and light truck tires
TechSight — monetary support
Llumar — monetary support and window tint
Mobil — lubricants and monetary support
Bosch — ignition parts and monetary support
PPG — monetary support for paintwork
Eibach — special rally springs
Bilstein — special rally shock absorbers
Hella — driving lights
Optima — car battery
American Sign Shops — graphics
Nutribiotics — power bars
Nikon — cameras
Toad Hall Books — monetary and moral support

Index